Praise *for Shake the World*

"At Zappos, one of our core values is to 'Embrace and Drive Change.' This book is for anyone interested in inspiring their own life to change for the better, both personally and professionally!"

—Tony Hsieh, *New York Times* bestselling author of

"Charity: water was founded out of a desire to inspire a new generation of givers to solve the water crisis. In this book, James introduces you to many of our friends who had the fearlessness to break the mold and think incredibly big. Prepare to be inspired, and then to act!"

—Scott Harrison, founder and CEO of charity: water

"A new generation wants work to be about far more than making money—they want their jobs to make a positive difference to the world. James Marshall Reilly has written a compelling and optimistic first-hand account of what it means to put this excellent goal into practice."

—Matthew Bishop, New York bureau chief of *The Economist* and coauthor of *Philanthrocapitalism: How Giving Can Save the World*

"James is able to bring people together who can solve real problems, and has an energy that inspires others to do the same."

—Stefan Weitz, director of Bing

"It's an eye-opening book 'not about finding a job, but about creating a life' that all high school and college kids should read to help them think outside the last-century box in this new millennium. . . . That's one recurring theme of *Shake the World*, a hot new book . . . about a growing number of young . . . socially conscious entrepreneurs who, in an age of avarice, measure their own success by how much they give back."

—*New York Daily News*

"Forget triple-bottom-line companies. James Marshall Reilly documents triple-bottom-line individuals—a cadre of brilliant business adventurers devoted to building a better world and—just as importantly—finding a better way to live in that world. With great storytelling and penetrating insight, *Shake the World* adds an entrepreneurial twist to the quest for the meaning of life."

—Steven Kotler, bestselling author of *Abundance*,
A Small Furry Prayer, and *West of Jesus*

"A quick and informative read."   —*Men's Fitness*

"Top Five Book of the Year . . . Reilly is eloquent as no one else about the existential crisis of (Western) youth today. . . . Upliftingly cool!"

—*Science of the Time*

"Studded with inspirational gems."   —*Kirkus Reviews*

"It's a grim time out there with millions of unemployed or underemployed, out of work for months if not years, whether newly minted college graduates or corporate veterans. Having interviewed a good handful of entrepreneurs (as well as drawing on his own youthful success . . .), Reilly is ready to share his take on what makes career changers succeed. . . . [H]is enthusiasm and spirit are contagious and might just provide a good boost to the weary job seeker."   —*Booklist*

"What I got out of reading this book is that it's never too late to shift your mind-set about how the world works. Read *Shake the World* and see what lessons you can put into practice for your own life and your business."   —*Small Business Trends*

"If you need proof that the generation now entering the workforce is motivated increasingly by improving the world as much as by making money, this book provides plenty of it." —Philanthrocapitalism.net

"As brilliantly documented in James Marshall Reilly's book, *Shake the World: It's Not About Finding a Job, It's About Creating a Life*, Millennials are busy changing h~~ow~~

—Don Tapscott, coauthor of *Macrowikinomics: Rebooting Business and the World*

"I highly recommend the idea-filled and engaging book *Shake the World: It's Not About Finding a Job, It's About Creating a Life* by James Marshall Reilly to anyone seeking a blueprint for success that goes beyond the standard success manuals. This book provides a foundation for building a wonderful new world and for establishing a meaningful life of purpose within that new world as well."

—Wayne Hurlbert, BlogTalkRadio host

"This book shifts the mind-set for anyone who reads it. Define your own success and then do what the best have already done to achieve it. Reilly has uncovered the secrets of the most hyper-successful people of this generation. If you internalize their lessons you will accelerate the rate at which you achieve the success goals you have for yourself."

—Cameron Herold, author *of Double Double* and former COO of 1-800-GOT-JUNK?

ABOUT THE AUTHOR

James Marshall Reilly is an entrepreneur, consultant, journalist, public speaker, and the founder of The Guild Agency Speakers Bureau & Intellectual Talent Management, Inc., a smart-content media firm headquartered in New York City. His work is focused on the branding and marketing of cutting-edge thinkers and connecting them with audiences worldwide, exclusively representing and advising numerous world-class business leaders, entrepreneurs, best-selling authors, philanthropists, and global-thought leaders. He has lectured at corporations, universities, and conferences in North America and Europe, including Microsoft, Syngenta, M.I.T., and Chicago Ideas Week. In 2011 Reilly was honored at the White House as one of the top 100 entrepreneurs in the United States age thirty or under. He currently resides in New York City.

Visit www.shaketheworldbook.com.

SHAKE THE

WORLD

It's Not About Finding a Job, It's About Creating a Life

JAMES MARSHALL REILLY

PORTFOLIO / PENGUIN

PORTFOLIO / PENGUIN
Published by the Penguin Group
Penguin Group (USA) Inc., 375 Hudson Street,
New York, New York 10014, USA

USA | Canada | UK | Ireland | Australia | New Zealand | India | South Africa | China
Penguin Books Ltd, Registered Offices: 80 Strand, London WC2R 0RL, England
For more information about the Penguin Group visit penguin.com

First published in the United States of America by Portfolio/Penguin,
a member of Penguin Group (USA) Inc., 2011
This paperback edition with a new foreword published 2013

THE LIBRARY OF CONGRESS HAS CATALOGED THE HARDCOVER EDITION AS FOLLOWS:
Reilly, James Marshall.
Shake the world : it's not about finding a job, it's about creating a life /
James Marshall Reilly.
p. cm.
Includes bibliographical references and index.
ISBN 978-1-59184-455-6 (hc.)
ISBN 978-1-59184-655-0 (pbk.)
1. Job hunting. 2. Success. I. Title.
HF5382.7.R45 2012
650.14—dc23

Printed in the United States of America
1   3   5   7   9   10   8   6   4   2

Set in Minion Pro
Designed by Lucy Albanese

8

CHANNELING PASSION

10

LEVERAGING FAILURE

It's funny what we remember. When I was about thirty years old, I lost a number of years to Lyme disease. In the early part of that illness, there were these phantom pains—shooting, stabbing, totally discombobulating, and out of freaking nowhere. One minute I'd be walking across my Los Angeles apartment, the next I'd be laying on the ground, moaning. There was a lot of moaning back then. Also a lot of dust. Our apartment had louvered windows and there's tons of dust in LA. It blew in off the street and settled on the floor and, as I wrote in *West of Jesus*, I spent much of that time with T.S. Eliot's line "I will show you fear in a handful of dust" stuck in my head.

As I said, it's funny what we remember.

Another thing that has stayed stuck in my head from those years comes from the opening line in the movie *Confessions of a Dangerous Mind*: "When you're young, your potential is infinite. You might do anything, really. You might be Einstein, you might be DiMaggio. Then you get to an age when what you might be gives way to what you have been. You weren't Einstein. You weren't anything. That's a bad moment."

I think, after three years in bed, the reason this quote was stuck in my head is pretty self-explanatory, but that's not why I'm bringing it up. I mention it here because James Marshall Reilly's *Shake the World* is a book about people who have avoided that "bad moment," and it's a handbook for anyone wondering how to do the same—and that's no small thing.

What's funny about the desire to avoid that bad moment is it's actually hardwired into our genes. All of us have a natural instinct to shake the world. Thanks to evolution's relentless need for innovation, we are literally programmed for the desire. Psychologists call this our *third drive*—a blend of autonomy (the desire to control our own fate), mastery (the desire to get better at what we do) and purpose (the desire to be part of something greater than ourselves). And it's a powerful drive. After basic survival needs have been met, as now hundreds of studies have shown, these three intrinsic desires are what motivate us most.

And mostly that's good news. The bad news is that world-changing ambition doesn't come with a guidebook. This isn't exactly paint by numbers. And without any kind of map, we want to shake the world but don't know how to shake the world—and you know how this goes, pretty soon we've settled for writing a blog.

And for those people who don't want to settle? Well, James Marshall Reilly's *Shake the World* is also that guidebook. It's a book about entrepreneurship and ethics, about using business as a force for good, and about what it takes to use business as a force for good. The leaders profiled in the book are ordinary folk who have leveraged technology, elevated compassion, and figured out how to put shoes on a million barefoot kids or feed tens of millions of hungry children. But the metastory here is that accomplishments like these—fundamental, leave-the-world-a-better-place-than-you-found-it accomplishments—are all within our power.

In *Abundance*, a book I cowrote with Peter Diamandis, we document four emerging forces that allow us to significantly increase global standards of living over the next few decades. But *Abundance* is not a book about techno-optimism. The challenges we face are great and the changes we outline will not happen automatically. Of those four forces, one is technological and the other three are biological—they're human in origin. Th

...................., in light of what's possible and the gravity of our situation, it couldn't have arrived at a better time.

Steven Kotler
April 2013

I N EARLY DECEMBER of 2009, I was in the Benjamin Franklin Room at the U.S. State Department with roughly one hundred other people waiting for Secretary of State Hillary Rodham Clinton to take her place at the microphone. Sitting about ten feet from the podium and typing furiously on my BlackBerry, I glanced up and noticed Wyclef Jean, who, in a few hours, would be hopping on a plane to Oslo for President Obama's acceptance of the Nobel Peace Prize. As I fidgeted in my seat, a Haitian diplomat was practically sitting on my lap (not intentionally, I'm fairly certain), and I couldn't help but smile as I scanned the room and saw a few friends and colleagues peppered throughout the audience.

You'd think they'd put more comfortable chairs in a place like the State Department, I thought to myself, trying to decide whether or not I should tweet this sentiment. Although I had been invited to this event to watch one of the people I worked with receive a humanitarian award, after spending the better part of the early evening surrounded by dignitaries and a diverse group of staggeringly accomplished individuals, my thoughts became consumed by one overriding, self-reflective question. *How on earth did I get here?*

In a world where recent college graduates were working as unpaid interns or in low-paying positions, where many of my peers were living with their parents or shacking up with multiple roommates while they looked for any job they could get, I felt very fortunate. At the time, the economic climate was such that many of those who had been part of the conventional workforce for years were feeling expendable, and people of all ages were taking jobs simply to keep a seat warm or to pay the bills.

I have an English degree from a university that most people have never heard of, located so deep in upstate New York that my default description in social situations is, "It's right next to Canada." I took a seemingly absurd path for the first few years after college, which included performing over six hundred concerts during a three-and-a-half-year stretch with a band you've never heard of (that's over two hundred nights a year on the road and roughly 250,000 miles of driving) and occasionally sharing the stage with Rock and Roll Hall of Famers and Grammy winners—but barely making enough money to do much more than eat and pay the rent—all while my close friends were attempting to build traditional careers or attending graduate school. So, I was compelled to wonder, How did I end up at the State Department with such an inspiring group of people?

When I walked away from the band, I stuck with what I knew and immediately started a small music management company. I attracted some great clients and quickly jettisoned into a fast-paced world of business and high-price, high-pressure negotiations, often acting on behalf of well-known artists who have sold out venues like Madison Square Garden and had albums at the top of the *Billboard* charts. Intrigued by how easy I found the transition from being in a band to running this new business, I decided to explore other possibilities.

I soon segued out of music when I had an opportunity to parlay my experience into a more intellectually stimulating job, this time working as an agent for Nobel and Pulitzer Prize winners as well as various well-known public figures and celebrities. Over the course of these collective

... least not on paper.

But what most of my friends didn't realize was that my band consisted of two small businesses, and I worked on those businesses twelve hours a day, seven days a week, for several years—beginning while I was still in college. I learned the ins and outs of contract negotiation, marketing, branding, advertising, management, and sales from the ground up, selling a "product" that no one had ever heard of. So when I had the opportunity to work with and represent highly sought after talent—names people actually *had* heard of—I found that my skills not only transferred seamlessly, but that it was quite easy for me to thrive.

Walking through the hallways of the State Department that day, surrounded by artifacts of American history in the Benjamin Franklin Room while simultaneously interacting with contemporary figures of living history—in awe of the diverse accomplishments and backgrounds of the people surrounding me—I became consumed with the concept of success. What it is and how we find it, both individually and collectively. And that got me thinking about something far more important than myself or how *I* got anywhere.

It occurred to me that it would be quite valuable for someone to conduct empirical research by speaking directly with the young game changers of this generation, those who are at the absolute top of their respective fields, in order to learn how *they* found success.

How do they define "success"?

How did they get where they are?

And can their paths be a template for others?

Several months later, I decided to do exactly that.

↜

WHEN I FIRST set out to execute this plan, I had no idea what to expect. I had just turned twenty-eight, and even though the financial crisis was in full swing, I had recently parted ways with a relatively cushy job where I wore jeans to work, came and went as I pleased, had a private office and an assistant, and worked with some of the most well-known public figures in the world. I had all of the traditional trappings of a "great" job, I lived in a beautiful area, and I had every material possession I thought I could ever want. But I was generally miserable—something was missing. Some of my friends, the same friends who had taken traditional career paths and a few of whom had been recently laid off, were now even more confused than before. I had seemingly done everything wrong, yet somehow I had landed exactly where they thought they wanted to be. And I was leaving it all behind.

As a writer, I now had to determine how to approach an entirely new space. I needed to identify top business and thought leaders from this generation, and then convince them to actually talk to me. From these conversations my intent was to gain insight into the future of business and the seismic shifts in the job market—which are far more significant, systemic, far-reaching, and long-standing than fluctuating unemployment statistics might indicate at any given time—then extract universal success tenets that I hoped would resonate with others. While there was no shortage of obstacles in front of me, I knew one thing for certain.

This was not going to be a book about finding a job.
It was going to be a book about creating a life.

As one subset of the workforce attempts to navigate old corporate
America in an effort to mak...

...ng paradigms while
...multaneously altering the force and direction of capitalism as it creates a global, borderless, highly profitable, often green and philanthropic, sustainable twenty-first-century economy that will provide the
jobs, careers, lifestyles, and opportunities for success, however we may
define it, for our collective futures. So, as I sat in that very uncomfortable chair at the State Department, and later that evening as I stood
shoulder to shoulder with some of the brightest of this generation, I
came to the conclusion that it would be invaluable for the rest of us if
we could answer one critical question.

Is there a new blueprint for success?

⌇

OVER THE COURSE of the following year, I interviewed and spent time
with some of the top young entrepreneurs, business owners, technology
experts, educators, artists, and philanthropists in America—the very
people who are shaping our future in every sense of the word. I traveled
to their corporate headquarters and met with them in their homes,
learning and observing all the while. I spoke with the founders and
CEOs of both privately held and publicly traded companies. I interviewed groundbreaking humanitarians and social entrepreneurs. I met

with best-selling authors, representatives from the United Nations and the United Nations Foundation, shared dinners and attended events with highly respected thought leaders, and shadowed individuals conducting world-changing work of epic proportion. A number are spearheading nonprofit initiatives both at home in the United States and in some of the most disparate countries and regions of the world—including Uganda, Laos, parts of South America, Haiti, and the Democratic Republic of the Congo—while others are building strictly for-profit companies defined by a new corporate ethos. A few have been able to strategically combine both profit and philanthropy in entirely unique ways. All of them are initiating change, not through old-school business models or established channels but by harnessing twenty-first-century technology coupled with cutting-edge ideation as they create and participate in new marketplaces. In the process, every one of them has built a life that is marked by almost immeasurable success.

The lives and careers of the men and women showcased in this book began just like anyone else's. Some of them grew up privileged, others came from middle- or working-class backgrounds—and their diversity is not confined to gender or socioeconomic upbringing. It is geographic, educational, ethnic, racial, and philosophic. Many were born in the United States, some emigrated from other countries. A few were raised in rural communities. Others grew up in or near large cities. Some attended top schools, and a couple dropped out of college. A few earned advanced degrees. Some of them now run for-profit companies, while others head nonprofit initiatives. A few work for or founded large global corporations. Others are completely immersed in small start-up enterprises that they built themselves. In some cases these endeavors were funded by entrepreneurs with access to millions of dollars, whereas in others the only start-up capital was the change in their pockets and the shirts on their backs.

There is no denying that the lives of these individuals have turned out very differently from most. Some have founded and then sold companies for staggering amounts of money. Others have revolutionized industries, completed heroic acts of self-sacrifice, and made inroads in corporate leadership, education, finance, banking, global politics, and human rights. Some have worked to fight poverty, alleviate hunger, advance nutrition, and eradicate disease. As a group, they have enacted substantial change. For many of the...

...by the sheer magnitude of their accomplishments, I found each of them to be humbled by their own experiences as well. I could feel the humility resonate in their voices when we spoke, and I could hear it echo, again and again, in my head as I compiled their stories. All of them are smart and innovative thinkers. Every one of them has achieved remarkable success, often by a surprisingly young age. And while every one of them achieved it differently, these individuals have all worked exceptionally hard, struggling at times to find their way. They have faced challenges, weathered setbacks, and met face-to-face with flat-out failure.

One of the observations that I made as I dissected the lives and stories of these extraordinary young people was that beneath all of their success, in many respects, and in the most positive sense of the word, they are surprisingly *ordinary*. In more ways than not, I found them to be just like the rest of us—they just happen to engage differently with the world around them. And while they would likely be the first to acknowledge this fact, it was this core observation that propelled me to think about success from a completely new perspective.

When I considered that success may not be solely predetermined for the fortunate few who are singularly brilliant, fortuitously positioned, or "in the right place at the right time," it opened up the possibility that there are specific behaviors we can all engage in that will help us cultivate success for ourselves. On our own terms. What I found is that there are many traits and behavior patterns these visionary young people have in common that can be used as a template to help others cultivate success in their own lives. If what seems to come so naturally to a select few can be learned by the rest of us, then perhaps we can draft a universal blueprint for success. And one that works in the rapidly evolving marketplace. One we can execute regardless of where we started out or went to school, no matter what year we were born or who our parents are, no matter what we majored in, what we seek to accomplish, or how often we have failed.

What I observed by observing the successful is that success can potentially be honed and crafted by anyone.

This group of enormously accomplished, and in some cases seemingly unreachable, leaders and visionaries were all kind, forthcoming, and generous as they opened their doors and patiently recounted their stories to me. I spoke with them about everything from how they found their way, to their vision for the future, to their respective definitions of "life," "work," and "success." Every one of them has a life and a story worthy of more than the few pages I have written here—in fact, a few have already written books of their own. And while I had to whittle down their extraordinary journeys to fit within the confines of just a few pages, it was without question a struggle to do so. Success of this magnitude can be difficult to squeeze into a small space. My only hope is that each reader can glean as much from these brilliant individuals and their innovative enterprises as I did in observing and writing about them.

These are some of the foremost leaders from this generation who have achieved extraordinary success.

And this is what they told me.

1

The Experience MBA, a Knowledge-Based GPS,
and a Lifetime of Extraordinary Responses

■

I have never let my schooling interfere with my
education.

—MARK TWAIN

A S THE FIRST decade of the twenty-first century began to
wind down, banks failed at the highest rate since the Great
Depression, giant American corporations including Lehman Brothers, Chrysler, and General Motors filed for bankruptcy, the housing market collapsed, and unemployment soared to near-record rates. Washington responded by providing billions of dollars in corporate bailouts and an economic stimulus package that, for the most part, wasn't successful in generating sustainable jobs—at least not in the short term.

Stock and commodity markets slumped worldwide, credit froze, and pension funds evaporated, culminating in a loss, on a global level, of trillions of dollars in both corporate and private wealth. Adding insult to injury, fraudulent hedge fund managers shook both Wall Street and Main Street with billion-dollar Ponzi schemes that spread like the Street's own viral form of swine flu. A few years later, as we sat poised on the brink of recovery from what appeared to be a free-market economic collapse, young people were confronted with what continued to be, for them, a residual and apocalyptic prospect.

There were still no jobs.

Although college and university attendance had reached record numbers, with over 70 percent of 2009 high school graduates enrolled in institutions of higher learning,[1] young people, even those with an advanced level of education, were facing one of the highest rates of unemployment since the government began collecting this data in 1948. For many, that very expensive college diploma suddenly seemed no better than one of those participation trophies that are handed out in youth sports just for showing up.

Everyone may get one, but they are basically worthless.

Despite being saddled, in some cases, with five- and six-figure student loans, any expectation many new graduates had for a Wall Street-sized salary—or any salary for that matter—had simply evaporated, seemingly overnight. They might have had résumés that would have garnered dream jobs just a few years back, but those résumés now landed them among the ranks of the woefully unemployed or underemployed— leaving a large number of young people painfully disenfranchised. As

1. http://www.bls.gov/news.release/hsgec.nr0.htm Bureau of Labor Statistics, April 27, 2010.

long-term plans made way for short-term necessity, they set out in droves to do what would have been, just a few years earlier, unthinkable.

They began their careers by working for free.

. . . . And the reason this occurred was due only in part to the poor economy.

The college internship, which had evolved into a popular and valuable tool for acquiring résumé- and skill-building, real-world work experience while generating credit for undergraduates, ended up playing a significant role in fundamentally changing the job market. For students, an internship often required a commitment of only a few hours a week or was undertaken in lieu of a summer job. But when the economy fell apart in 2008 and unemployment rates soared, the unpaid internship spread—becoming so prevalent that it functioned to replace the entry-level job for a large number of college graduates. Because so many companies were cutting their labor force—the job supply was low and demand was extremely high—many employers saw an opportunity to take advantage of this very cheap labor pool by extending the concept of the student internship into the postgraduate job market. And a lot of them did, simply by reducing the compensation offered to new hires. Sometimes all the way to zero.

As a result, many new graduates found themselves fiercely competing for unpaid, or very low-paying, full-time internships. Some of these were classified as "temp positions," offering no benefits and compensation near minimum wage—a distinction that allowed companies to circumvent official corporate hiring freezes. Regardless of what they were called, these were essentially the same positions that just a few years before would have been entry-level jobs that came with valuable training, full benefits, and a competitive salary. When concerns were raised about this emerging trend, many state governments responded by mandating that these internships be regulated with minimum standards. This helped a little, but there was no question that the job market had found a new bottom.

It was not uncommon for young people with degrees from respected four-year schools to hold jobs that, in terms of income, resulted in a net loss. Even after going into debt to pay for college, some found themselves going even further into debt in order to secure employment as well. Since the internship was a familiar and often very positive experience from their college days and career prospects were so poor, many young people segued right into these positions after graduation with optimism and gratitude. These were positions that often didn't pay enough to cover commuting costs, self-paid health insurance premiums, and basic clothes for work—let alone rent. The part-time college internship for experience or course credit became the unpaid internship after graduation, and that evolved into the low-paying internship when the government stepped in. But the bottom line was that, for many entering the workforce, it replaced what used to be the entry-level job. And it was a phenomenon that represented a corporate, economic, and sociological shift of gargantuan proportions.

Because it was a marker that signified
that all the rules had changed.

With such a large number of educated people entering the market desperate for *any* job, the corporations offering these positions gained a substantial amount of power. There was an endless line out the door of qualified and even overqualified applicants, companies didn't have to pay new employees much or provide benefits, and this often meant that they didn't necessarily have a lot vested in the success of these new hires either. These new employees were, in many cases, completely replaceable—which encouraged a revolving-door employment culture at many companies. Even so, these positions were so highly sought after that internship-search companies were charging fees, frequently upward of a thousand dollars, to find suitable placements.

...created young labor pool available to work for free, or for a disproportionately small stipend, it became exponentially more difficult for everyone else to find employment.

While some of these internships were nothing more than companies exploiting free or nearly free labor, many others came with extremely valuable training. Either way, recent graduates felt pressured to figure out how to make these postgraduate internships work, since they had become a necessary gateway to paid positions. They almost always came sweetened with the promise of a potential "real" job down the road, but regardless of whether that actually panned out, real-world work experience by way of an internship was now critical to have on a résumé.

The postgraduate internship had become the "Experience MBA."

What started out as a part-time opportunity to gain experience and earn college credit for undergraduate students ended up fundamentally changing the landscape of the job market—and not just at the entry-level tier. Experienced members of the workforce were affected as well. The *New York Times* reported a story in November of 2009 in which a thirty-eight-year-old lost his job at Bear Stearns and found himself unable to secure a new position, so he decided to "intern" for a wealth management company. Even though he offered to work for free, the company ended up paying him ten dollars an hour—a far cry from his old salary at Bear Stearns. Despite not being offered a permanent position after five months, he still felt that he gained valuable training and skills that would help him land a paid position somewhere else.

The dynamics within the career marketplace had shifted so drastically that a trained professional with over a decade of experience and a family to support was *grateful* to work for a few dollars over minimum wage. Companies now had an "internship option," allowing them to put off hiring seasoned workers by hiring interns instead. These interns may not have been as experienced—and they weren't necessarily as qualified—but the price was right. This type of economic competition within the job market had typically only involved work that was outsourced to foreign countries where labor is significantly cheaper—but this wasn't happening overseas. This time it was happening right here at home. The availability of this labor pool changed the fundamentals of the entire job market by shifting the power structure, establishing a new entry-level tier that, even in cases where the internship *was* a fantastic learning experience and *did* lead to a great job down the line, could be both logistically and financially difficult—or impossible—for many to navigate.

> *As game-changing as this was, this single and seemingly innocuous concept—the creation of low-paying, résumé-building, experience-generating internships for college graduates—was only one part of an even broader shift in the job market.*

⌒

WE ARE MEMBERS of the first generation armed with far more than *just* a college degree. The knowledge we gained from courses we took in economics, government, statistics, communications, global or public policy, technology, or literature pale in comparison to the education we have cultivated outside the brick and ivy-covered buildings of the traditional academic institutions that awarded us diplomas—and not just as a result of the real-world

...gh speed, fast-paced, new-tech borderless world like it's an old dirt road from our collective childhood. Because it is. Young people today have a built-in navigation system: a cultural, business, social, political, and knowledge-based GPS.

For us it's just normal. We have reached a comfort zone where we adapt in a rapid-fire fashion to technological change as our bosses and potential employers, sometimes just a few years our elder, often find themselves lost in our techno-information vapor trail. This gives us a distinct competitive advantage, and frankly it makes us, as a generation, *different*. We are social-media gourmands with skill sets that *should* manifest to give us exceptional power in the workplace and the world around us. Yet most of us don't even realize this, let alone know how to capitalize on it. With our ability to quickly adapt to changing technology, we are genuinely empowered. Our connectivity renders us informed and confident. And why not? There is virtually nothing that we can't find out—almost immediately, without much effort, and for free.

> *The traditional gatekeepers of information are no longer the only ones holding the keys.*

And the shift in power doesn't end with the access we now have to what was once proprietary information—whether educational or industry-specific. We can literally roam the world from the palm of our hand. We can read, see, and almost taste the change happening around the globe. And many of us want to be part of it. Starting a multi-million-dollar company from your dorm room? Becoming a serial entrepreneur? Facilitating hundreds of millions of dollars in micro-loans to lift people out of poverty in developing nations? Building schools to provide access to education? Distributing millions of mosquito nets in malaria-ridden regions of Africa? Branding a whistle as an international symbol of injustice? Building a billion-dollar corporation in a counterintuitive manner? And accomplishing this by challenging existing paradigms and established norms? No matter where our interests lie, these are the opportunities that have been afforded to our generation. It has never been easier to execute whatever it is we might want to accomplish—it simply requires pushing past a few barriers.

Historically, a poor job market is an accelerant for entrepreneurship. Many well-known corporations including General Motors, Revlon, Disney, and Microsoft were started during times of economic hardship. So it should not be unexpected that as an addendum to the poor economy, high unemployment, and the new Experience MBA, with its resultant tier of low-paying entry-level jobs, there is a subgroup of this generation who are successfully starting their own companies or running enterprises that capitalize on all of this change. They are representative of a new breed of leaders who are manufacturing innovative and tangible results—inventing new markets and forms of currency as they build companies or organizations with dynamic culture and well-paying positions that often come with enormous self-affirming dividends. As a result, they are creating the jobs that most of us would find much more rewarding than "pushing paper" in the traditional nine-to-five corporate space, especially in a world where paper is something that many of us have hardly used in years.

In the history of the job market, there has never been such a transformational time. There have been enormous changes in education, technological advances, a sociological and ideological shift in hiring practices and personal career-based expectations, as well as burgeoning new industries that have collectively and fundamentally altered the landscape for the future of employment. And unlike temporary unemployment numbers and fall ͫ ᷄

CHAD TROUTWINE COFOUNDED and owns the largest privately held Graduate Management Admission Test (GMAT) preparation company in the world. His company, Veritas Prep, was developed from a business concept that he incubated while attending graduate school at Yale University. One of Troutwine's friends had dropped out of the University of Southern California to start an LSAT (Law School Admission Test) prep company, and the idea inspired him. "I admired him so much. I couldn't help but feel that there wasn't a similar opportunity in the GMAT space," Chad tells me as we walk along an ocean-side road in Malibu, California, just a stone's throw away from his rooftop corporate headquarters near Pepperdine University. Troutwine's concept and business plan for Veritas Prep won several competitions, and while he was still in graduate school developing the idea he was named Young Entrepreneur of the Year by *Forbes* magazine. Chad and his business partner, Markus Moberg, used the prize money from the different competitions they won to fund the company during Chad's final semester at Yale. "We just dove in," he tells me. "We practically dropped out our last semester."

On average, Veritas Prep increases students' test scores by 120 points. Troutwine attributes this to both the rigorous screening process for their instructors—each has scored in the 99th percentile or above on an actual GMAT exam—and a constantly evolving, cutting-edge curriculum.

Classes are offered in roughly one hundred cities as well as online, and Veritas Prep has been featured or referenced in publications that include the *Wall Street Journal*, the *New York Times*, *USA Today*, and *Business-Week*, to name a few.

"Veritas was an opportunity to take on a duopoly," Chad tells me. "Kaplan's and the Princeton Review's standards have gone down, prices have gone up, and they are just taking advantage of the system to gouge. So we went after them," he says. "It wasn't Google that invented search, they just came up with a better design and made it more user-friendly," Chad explains. And this is how he views Veritas Prep—a test preparation company focused on the user. "What we offer has a great lasting benefit, which we're very proud of. We're obsessed with the perfect course, basically regardless of the bottom line. The best gift we can give someone is twenty extra points on their test to help them get into their dream school."

Veritas Prep will service roughly ten thousand clients in 2010 according to Chad. "We're still small—we'll still be under twenty-five million dollars this year, so in terms of revenue that's a smaller company—and it's very manageable, and we're on to something that we're very proud of," he tells me. Yet despite owning a company that specializes in graduate school test preparation and holding an MBA from Yale University School of Management, Chad thinks that for many people, pursuing an MBA—especially in this day and age—can be a potentially fatal mistake.

"There are more than two thousand institutions in the United States that confer an MBA," Chad tells me as we sit down at a lunch spot just off the beach. "By comparison, there are only about a hundred and eighty accredited law schools and only about a hundred and ten accredited medical schools. Is the average MBA candidate at a school that's not ranked in the top twenty or thirty in the country really better off?" he asks. "Because the tuition isn't much different."

Chad goes on to address the fact that many individuals pursue advanced degrees on a part-time basis. "Now, there are some people who are going to extract information from these programs, and that's great. Maybe they'll make connections—who knows? Maybe one of their classmates is someone they'll end up launching a business with

For some people ..."

... people who receive an MBA from a school or program not in the top tier. Chad proceeds to give me a hypothetical example—this is coming from the perspective of someone who employs over five hundred individuals at Veritas Prep, a company that exists for the purpose of helping people get into graduate schools and generates millions of dollars in revenue each year doing so.

"Let's say that I'm looking at two candidates for a position, and let's say that they are both in their late twenties. Both candidates went to UCLA for their undergraduate degrees—a good public school, a 'public Ivy.' Same major, same GPA. If one of them has an MBA from a lower-tier school, in some ways I might think less of that candidate than the one who lacks an MBA, because the first person *chose* a lower-tier MBA program—that almost dings their résumé in some ways. It's not out of elitism," he is quick to point out. Rather, it is a question of value, experience, and opportunity cost. "What little bit of knowledge that person may have gained in that program still takes a hit on the 'was that really a good decision?' part," he explains.

We discuss the fact that with the educational tools and information readily available from sources outside of colleges and universities, during the few years that the first hypothetical candidate was studying for the entrance exam, spending money or going into debt to cover tuition expenses, and actually working toward earning an MBA, the second candidate could have developed a few years of practical business experience. "The person who didn't take the MBA route has likely spent time in the real world," Chad reinforces. As an employer, he views this metric as "a signaling device." If an individual made the decision to go to a mid-tier business school, it is an indication that they don't *necessarily* make the best decisions. "Experience trumps a piece of paper," he tells me.

Troutwine, who has produced several films, including *Paris, je t'aime*, was in the process of releasing his most recent project, *Freakonomics*, based on the best-selling book of the same name, when we spoke. *Freakonomics* debuted at the Tribeca Film Festival and was screened at Cannes, the Los Angeles Film Festival, and the Toronto Film Festival as well. Two hours after our interview he would be getting on a plane to the East Coast to make the cable television rounds and then departing for Europe to promote the film's release. He cites an example based on a comment made years ago by then first-time writer-director Quentin Tarantino. "When Tarantino premiered *Reservoir Dogs* at the Sundance Film Festival, he was the darling. He would sit on these panels, and the same questions would keep coming up at each event. 'Tell us about your background. Where did you go to film school?' And his answer was always the same. 'I didn't go to film school. I went to films.'"

Experience trumps a piece of paper.

In regard to undergraduate education, Chad identifies what he perceives to be flaws in the system. "One dangerous aspect about the increasing tuition at almost all these schools is that it's creating a quiet exclusion of groups," he tells me. "There are some groups who have the resources that will allow them to get an education—either they have wealthy parents, or perhaps they're fortunate enough to be someone who could be targeted for a scholarship. Then you have all kinds of groups who don't fall into those categories," he says. Chad is also quick to point out that there are areas of the country, including in the South and the rural Midwest, where he is from, where young people are "left behind" as a result of poor primary and secondary school education. "I went to a really bad public high school," he confesses.

We go on to di...

... have affects not only potential employers, but individuals as well. "People's perception of themselves, even if it's unfair, can be a hindrance," Chad says, emphasizing the fact that our self-identity is often a result of influencers that include where we are from, our socioeconomic background, what school we attended, and the like. Yet these are factors that may have little to do with skill or ability. When asked if the fictitious girl from Rutgers is necessarily any less qualified for a job than someone who went to an Ivy League school, he responds, "Often not."

Chad tells me that he doesn't like to make projections or predictions too far into the future but shares that he "thinks about education in the broader space constantly." And he isn't simply interested in GMAT testing and postgraduate studies. "I think there is going to be a continued migration away from the traditional university structure, and I think it's going to become weakened and beaten down on a variety of different fronts. I don't think there will be one 'thing' that replaces traditional college but rather a variety of different things. People will take a gap year with more frequency," he predicts, "and during that year they will mature and start considering other options.

"One of the pieces I haven't quite figured out yet is in regard to high school students making the decision about college," Chad says. "I wonder what role the parents will play in this. Will they be the last bastions of the old paradigms, ingraining in their children that 'this is the right path'?" he asks. Or will the children have the fortitude to choose their own path?"

From an employer's perspective, Chad asks one simple question. "Who would you rather be in the room with, someone who had their entire career figured out at eighteen and took classes in support of that career while an undergraduate, or someone who figures it out as they go?" Then he answers this question himself. "The second person is interesting."

It is time to reevaluate our traditional views on education,
both undergraduate and graduate, and then navigate the new
job market accordingly in order to gain both the knowledge
and the work experience necessary to be competitive.

∽

TOWARD THIS END, we can look for valuable internships and jobs, we can reassess the opportunity cost of higher education, and we can also self-educate as we gain essential and leverageable skill sets from outside the traditional spaces of work and school. But what I noticed in speaking with highly successful individuals like Chad is that there is an overarching step necessary for high achievement that can be implemented regardless of our educational background or work experience. And this necessitates engaging differently with the world around us in a very specific way.

Responding to relatively ordinary events
in an extraordinary manner.

Taking this step can facilitate life-altering success and can be accomplished even when we don't have what we might think is the necessary

education or any prerequisite experience in a particular field. As Chad
Troutwine suggests, many of the barriers to success lie in our own self-
imposed, perceived limitations. By disregarding the external labels and
expectations that have been bestowed upon us and by ignoring preconceived personal b

⟓

THE RICH SOIL of many tropical African countries, as well as areas in
northern India and Central America, contains microscopic pieces of
volcanic glass called silica. When absorbed through the skin, silica is
believed to cause a crippling fungal disease called podoconiosis, or
"Mossy Foot." This disease has a devastating effect on the lymphatic
system and manifests as disfiguring and painful swelling of the feet
(noninfectious geochemical elephantiasis), often followed by secondary
bacterial infections and keloids—thick scar tissue. Podoconiosis has
affected millions of people worldwide—over one million in Ethiopia
alone[2]—and there is no cure. It enters through the feet and is so devastating that it prevents those who have it from walking, working, and
going to school. It carries, along with the physical pain, an enormous
social stigma that often leads to those affected being ostracized by their
communities and abandoned by their families. As devastating and
prevalent as the disease is, podoconiosis can be completely prevented
by wearing a pair of shoes.

In 2006, while on vacation in Argentina, Blake Mycoskie wasn't

2. http://www.who.int/neglected_diseases/diseases/podoconiosis/en/index.html.

aware of podoconiosis. But he did become aware that many of the children he saw, barefoot and living in poverty, weren't allowed to attend school because they had no shoes. Astounded that youngsters were being denied the right to an education over something so seemingly basic as footwear, Blake decided to do something about it. He didn't work in education, he wasn't a doctor, and he didn't hold a degree in public health or own a shoe company. In fact, Blake had none of the traditional qualifications that *should* have allowed him to be equipped to address what is an issue of global health and education—or to manufacture footwear for that matter. Yet none of this deterred him.

What Blake had going for him was that he was an entrepreneur with a big heart and an extraordinary mind-set. He dropped out of Southern Methodist University years earlier after founding a successful campus laundry company, went on to start a variety of other businesses while in his twenties, and even competed on the television game show *The Amazing Race*. During the competition he briefly visited Argentina, and a few years later decided to return to take a break from his most recent business endeavor.

When Blake became aware that children were not permitted to attend school if they didn't own a pair of shoes, he became inspired to extend his stay in Argentina and, with a friend, hand make 250 pairs of traditional Argentine canvas shoes called *alpargatas*. He then returned home in hopes of selling the shoes to his family and friends. If he sold 250 pairs, he reasoned, he would not only have enough money to make another 250 pairs to give to children in Argentina who desperately needed them, but he would have enough money to make additional shoes to sell (which would, in turn, allow him to give more away). Blake recognized the shoeless children in Argentina not as an impossible-to-solve humanitarian issue but as a problem that could have a relatively easy, sustainable fix. One that, once addressed, could have enormous lifelong ramifications.

Blake's extraordinary response led him to found a company called TOMS. The company's credo is simple, and you've likely heard it: "With every pair you purchase, TOMS will give a pair of new shoes to a child in need. One for One." You might recognize TOMS for their fashion-

p ... and counting. And not only in Argentina but in podoconiosis-affected Ethiopia and many other countries as well.

"The funny thing about starting a new business, or really any new project, for that matter, is that the most valuable interns and employees are sometimes the ones that have the *least* experience in what you're trying to accomplish," Blake tells me. Quick to note the difference between established channels and paradigms and the new line of thinking that many entrepreneurs and businesses are embracing, he follows with a new-world example. "If you're following a set path, it makes sense to hire people that have seen and done what you're trying to do; but with new and innovative ideas, there is no 'right way' of doing things, and when the path to success is unclear, the worst thing that you can have are preconceived notions." TOMS is a prime example of the shifting needs of employers within the "innovative ideas" marketplace to which Blake is referring.

"When I was first starting TOMS, I pitched the idea to a college professor who said that I would need a *million dollars* to get the company off the ground," Blake says. "I spoke with veterans in the shoe industry who saw every reason why the idea would fail. 'The math just doesn't work' they would say, or 'the retail business is dying,' or 'there's no market for canvas slip-ons,' and on and on." Blake was quick to challenge these notions, seeking to establish a new route to solve an ongoing problem by creating a unique model for giving.

"At the time, TOMS was composed of myself, a few duffel bags of samples, a polo instructor pretending to be a shoemaker, and a handful of interns that I hired off of Craigslist. The idea was crazy," he emphasizes, "but my interns didn't know that. All they knew was that we were having fun, and that with a little creativity and resourcefulness, we could accomplish just about anything. As TOMS has grown, we've continued to look for these same traits in the interns and employees that we hire."

For Blake and the TOMS team, these characteristics are the key to building a successful group of like-minded individuals and, in turn, creating a successful brand and culture. To this end he asks, with emphasis, *"Are you passionate? Can you creatively solve problems? Can you be resourceful without resources? Do you have the compassion to serve others?* You can teach a new hire just about any skill," he tells me, "but you absolutely cannot inspire creativity and passion in someone that doesn't have it."

Upon returning from Argentina, Blake hired several interns and asked them to work out of his Venice, California, apartment—hardly a typical request from an employer. But after a *Los Angeles Times* feature about the fledgling company, he was forced to scramble as thousands of orders poured in from readers who became moved by the story. The problem was that he had only his original batch of 250 pairs of shoes, minus the few dozen he had already sold. He needed to quickly build a team to respond to the incoming orders while he returned to Argentina to make more shoes. It is clear that from the beginning Blake and the TOMS team took a different approach from most companies, creating a unique culture even when it was just he and a few interns trying to fill orders and keep the business moving forward.

"What every great company culture has in common is that everyone—from senior executives to interns starting their first day—feels like they're a part of something and that their efforts are contributing to a larger mission. Since our early apartment days," Blake tells me, "I've tried to create this culture by emphasizing trust. Trust comes from believing in others. It means giving people more responsibility than they've ever had, abandoning narrow job descriptions, and

...stay true to this mind-set. What allows us to keep giving away shoes is being profitable, and this is something that every intern and employee contributes to with every decision that they make," he says, emphasizing a palpable difference between traditional companies and the emerging model that many of the most forward-thinking and successful businesses of today are embracing. In Blake's case, he managed to innovate a unique coupling of profit and philanthropy through an easy-to-understand "One for One" model. At the time this was not a typical approach in the for-profit space, nor was it a typical model in the philanthropic space either.

"One of my favorite things about TOMS is giving the joy of giving to others," Blake tells me. And this is clearly obvious in the way in which the TOMS team approaches building experiences for their employees. "This is evident through our Shoe Drops, which are such an important part of our company culture that after the first full year of work, the company pays for employees to go to Argentina to meet my original partner, Alejo,[3] to see where the idea for TOMS started, and to hand place shoes on children's feet.

"The beauty of going on a Shoe Drop," Blake shares, "is that each person instantly feels how he or she is individually making a difference.

---

3. The "polo instructor pretending to be a shoemaker" that Blake referred to earlier.

Even though TOMS has many more people working in HQ (the company headquarters is based in Santa Monica, California), it's the individual work of every team member that has allowed us to give over one million new pairs of shoes. On a daily basis, we might feel stressed out, overloaded with e-mails, or tying up details that don't seem to matter," he says, "but they do matter, because all of our collective efforts make possible the true joy that comes from putting shoes on kids' feet."

Considering that Blake made the decision to drop out of college after the success of the campus laundry service he started, I wanted to know how he weighs academic experience against real-world experience and what traits he values in employees and partners. "The beauty of today's generation," he tells me, "is that you don't need fancy degrees, lots of resources, or special connections to start something that matters. Every one of us has the capacity to be a change maker; it just takes creativity and the willingness to continually face your fears." In regard to education, he echoes some of Chad Troutwine's earlier sentiments. "Can college be an incredible learning experience? Yes, it definitely can," Blake says, quickly adding, "but so can joining the Peace Corps, doing Teach for America, or just wholeheartedly going after what you're passionate about. Regardless of what path you take, I recommend that everyone work to cultivate creativity, passion, resourcefulness, and an entrepreneurial spirit. At the end of the day, these are the traits that will ultimately determine your success," he tells me, "and more importantly, the joy and personal fulfillment that you experience in life.

"Today's consumers (i.e., you and me) have so many options and are so distracted that it takes something special to get our attention," Blake says. "More than just buying stuff, we want to be a part of movements and surround ourselves with like-minded people that share our view of the world. As for today's generation, there's no doubt that we live in a unique time," he offers candidly. "With young people especially, I feel a cultural shift. The 'cool kids' on campus are now the ones supporting Invisible

Children and charity: water,[4] carrying their books in FEED bags, and organizing Style Your Sole[5] parties and barefoot walks for One Day Without Shoes.[6] This renewed social consciousness—combined with the power of technology to spread ideas—has definitely allowed TOMS to grow in a way that

[illegible faded text]

... to sell the 250 pairs that I had stuffed in my duffel bag. I consider myself an overly optimistic person, but never in my wildest dreams could I have imagined TOMS growing like it has," he confesses. "When I think about our success, the first thing that comes to mind is my TOMS family. Since the beginning apartment days, TOMS has been blessed with some of the smartest, most passionate, and most resourceful teams of employees and interns that I've ever met," Blake says. "Without every one of them, none of this crazy success would have been possible."

Blake's thoughts for the future are as applicable to TOMS as both a company and a movement as they are to any individual. "I hope that TOMS inspires young people to realize that making money and doing good don't have to be mutually exclusive," he offers in parting. "Start now. Tell great stories. Keep it simple. Do what you fear the most. Incorporate giving into everything that you do. Giving more might be the best business decision that you ever make."

---

4. http:// www.charitywater.org.
5. Parties in which groups of people create their own personalized designs on white canvas TOMS.
6. One Day Without Shoes takes place annually in early April and is designed to help people learn how most of the world lives by encouraging them to spend just one day without this basic item.

And when Blake says "business decision," he isn't necessarily refer-ring to starting one's own company—this concept is applicable to both entrepreneurs and conventional job seekers alike. This is a mind-set, a lifestyle, and an attitudinal barometer that reflects the zeitgeist of a tangible generational shift in the way we view the world and what we should expect from our pursuits, regardless of what they might be and regardless of how we individually define success. By shedding what we perceive to be all of the traditional barriers—all of the reasons why we *theoretically* can't—we might discover that we *actually* can.

Responding to relatively ordinary experiences and events in an extraordinary manner can drastically alter the trajectory of our lives and careers.

～

WHEN WE ANALYZE this story objectively, it is obvious that Blake should have had no particular reason to assume he would succeed. He had no experience in shoe manufacturing, no experience solving issues of global health and education, and no medical degree. Even his prior businesses (which included an outdoor advertising company and an online driving school) were completely unrelated to what he had set out to accomplish after visiting Argentina. What he *did* have when he approached this ven-ture was a uniquely cultivated entrepreneurial background and the mind-set that the traditional barriers of entry simply didn't apply. He set out to do something that was seemingly impossible: something for which he was, on paper, completely unqualified. And yet he found extraordinary success.

Blake's unique experience, his personal *success catalyst*, if you will, was that trip to Argentina and his encounter with the shoeless chil-dren. But we've all seen homeless people and starving children, footage from the tsunamis in Malaysia and Japan, the effects of Hurricane Katrina, and the devastation of the earthquakes in Haiti and Chile, just as examples.

Poverty and need are nothing new.

What is different about Blake's story is that he *acted* and, more importantly, that he did so in an *untraditional* way. He didn't turn a blind eye and he didn't

...for everyone if he could build a profitable business that could generate a parallel and self-perpetuating humanitarian by-product. A feel-good dividend for the consumer and access to an education and a healthier life for a child in a developing region. All in a pair of shoes.[7]

Extraordinary.

If we look at Blake's story with a more critical eye and even a dose of skepticism, it provides additional insight. We all know that many jobs and careers aren't open to people without a college degree. And income, one of the traditional markers of success, is typically correlated with level of education—the higher the education the higher the income, on average. But along with many well-known and extremely successful entrepreneurs and philanthropists, including Bill Gates and Ted Turner, Blake decided not to finish college.

7. In 2011, TOMS expanded their One for One model to include a line of eyewear in order to help restore eyesight to the millions of people around the globe who are suffering from blindness as a result of some form of correctable vision impairment, including cataracts. TOMS partnered with the Seva Foundation, and now every pair of TOMS sunglasses sold will provide a pair of prescription eyeglasses, medical treatment, or cataract surgery for a visually impaired person in Nepal, Cambodia, or Tibet. One for One.

Blake left school after his first company took off, undoubtedly knowing that dropping out of college isn't typically the best path to success but also that doing so doesn't necessarily preclude it. He made this decision because he perceived there was something even better for him to be doing with his time—and that proved to be the case. He didn't stay in school for the sake of staying in school, but, more importantly, he didn't drop out because he was lazy. People who drop out of school because they're lazy are probably not going to find success at anything because they dropped out of *trying*, not out of school. Success clearly doesn't occur without drive and hard work.

The conventional wisdom that dictated that Blake needed to stay in school and get a degree was something he was able to assess objectively in terms of his own personal circumstances, and then dismiss. He embraced this line of thinking over and over again as he started several companies throughout his twenties, and he continued this approach when he started TOMS—when a professor told him he would need a million dollars to launch the company, when he was told that there was "no market for canvas slip-ons," and when people insisted that the retail business was "dying." At each juncture when he was told a "truth," he ran it through his own internal filter and either accepted or rejected it—disregarding a lot of conventional thought along the way. The biggest difference between Blake and everyone else is the same difference that separates success from failure.

It's the ability to see beyond the conventional.
The ability to think and act differently.

The ability to respond to ordinary events
in an extraordinary way.

∽

WHAT CHAD TROUTWINE, Blake Mycoskie, and so many other young entrepreneurs indicate with regard to how they hire and whom they prefer to work with is that they *want* to see or hear about that ordinary experience that was responded to in an extraordinary manner because it signifies drive, determination, and, perhaps most importantly, the ability to think. *Differently.* Just like they do. They are looking for that

barrier, or nothing at all, we can create a far greater number of opportunities to succeed. This inclination eliminates restrictive thought and opens the gates traditionally locked by conventional "wisdom."

Twenty-first-century success is achieved when it is understood that many of the social and institutional barriers to entry encountered by past generations no longer apply. By summarily dismissing these perceived obstacles as irrelevant—if, in fact, they are—and responding to ordinary events in an extraordinary manner, we can create opportunities in the changing marketplace that are essential to the crafting of success in our own lives and careers.

> *We have landed in a new place. In terms of*
> *the job market. In terms of education. And in*
> *terms of how we should perceive limitations.*

2

PLAYING RISK

Naked Shorts, High-Beta Decisions,
and Generation "Why Not?"

∎

Only those who risk going too far can possibly
find out how far they can go.

—T. S. ELIOT

ONE OF THE riskiest moves a retail investor can make in the stock market is selling a stock short without owning an equal number of shares long. Selling a "naked short," as it is called, is a bearish move that involves borrowing someone else's shares and selling them at the current price with the intention of buying those shares back at a lower price at a later date to "cover" the open short position. The difference between what you paid for the borrowed shares you sold short, and what you end up paying for the shares you will later return, is your profit—or your loss—on that trade. The reason it is a bearish move is that you would only sell a naked short if you thought that particular stock was going to decline in value. And the reason it is dangerous is that, theoretically, your potential loss is unlimited.

Consider, for example, that if you buy a stock and own the shares long, the price of those shares can only fall to zero. In this case, you can actually calculate your potential worst-case scenario to the penny. In a catastrophic, lose-everything event, your risk exposure would simply be the cost of th [illegible] faced with what is called a "short squeeze." You would either be forced to buy the shares back and return them by covering your open position at the current, higher price to contain your loss, or face a margin call, requiring you to deposit additional cash into your account (if you don't already have enough) so that you will be able to meet your brokerage house's requirements *and* be better positioned to cover the cost of your short position if the trade continues to move against you. If you don't deposit the cash in time, the brokerage house starts indiscriminately selling off your long positions in other securities in order to raise the cash from your portfolio. Naked short selling is risky business indeed, and you need to have a high tolerance for risk to do it.

At any given time, risk is simply defined by what you have and what you have to lose. Luckily, in the stock market, you can actually calculate the risk-reward ratio of every trade you may want to make, often by simply tapping a few buttons on your mobile device. But not so in life. Risk assessment and risk tolerance for an individual's career are far more difficult to quantify. Career decisions play out over a long period of time, they are impacted by innumerable variables, and the options can't be backtested—though we do have to live with the results.

What happens if you're in college and you decide to major in economics rather than English? Or perhaps Russian history instead of art history? What if you take a semester abroad? Should it be in Italy or China? What are the metrics standing behind, and more importantly, *in front* of, these decisions? What if you take a year off from *whatever* it is that you are currently doing? Will it matter, and if so, in what ways? How does one calibrate and quantify risk-reward or opportunity cost when it comes to real life?

Say, for example, that when you graduate from college you decide to pass up a job or career opportunity, take on debt, and go to graduate school—what is the opportunity cost? What are the downside risks and the upside rewards of taking one job over another? Or what if you take on a different type of risk altogether and ask for a promotion at your current job but don't get it? What if you have the choice to switch departments at your company? Or leave your current job for a similar, but perhaps less secure, opportunity with higher pay and potentially better mobility at a higher-profile company? What are the complex risk and reward possibilities if you change jobs, or even careers, in midlife? Perhaps you're thinking about taking a similar job in another city, or maybe exploring a different field altogether, or even starting a new business of your own. Is a short-term risk going to turn into a long-term opportunity? The truth is that none of these risk assessments are easy to calculate. In fact, most of them are downright impossible.

Since the traders and analysts on Wall Street have made it their business to become masters of quantifying risk, at this point I'd like to hijack another term from the financial markets—"high-beta" stocks. High-beta stocks are simply the shares of companies whose stocks trade with above-average volatility—and like the twin peaks of a two-humped financial camel, these stocks carry both above-average risk and, potentially, above-average reward.

If you are a recent graduate, looking for a job, or simply trying to decide what to do next, you might believe that you are akin to a volatile high-beta stock—an awkward-looking mammal burdened with both extraordinary risk and, if you can *just* make all the right choices, potentially unlimited reward. And that's exactly why periods of career transition, like graduation or changing jobs, can be so stressful.

We don't want to make the wrong choice, yet the

.... they should be risk *averse* at the exact point when they should be risk *tolerant*.

So, where *is* the uncontained risk then? Where are the dreaded margin calls and those high-beta decisions you might want to avoid along your career trajectory? Where *are* the naked shorts of the job market? They are certainly coming later in your career, when you actually have something to lose. But when you are young and starting out? The simple answer is that there is only one fatal high-risk decision.

Selling yourself short.

Why?

Because you are already starting out at zero.

When you begin at zero, there is nowhere to go but up. At this juncture you are perfectly positioned for that meteoric rise. In other words, when you are young or fresh out of school, without much of anything to lose, it is the precise time that you should take a few chances. This is an ideal opportunity to take on what many might falsely assume is a high-risk career decision by taking advantage of that high-beta, *one-hump*, no-risk, all-reward situation.

Wall Street traders would call this reassessing your risk tolerance.

In fact, it is far more productive to rethink what you perceive to be risk and reframe it as opportunity. That same risk that might loom as catastrophically large down the road when you actually have something to lose, whether an existing career or lifestyle, perhaps your professional reputation or even your life savings, is, for a small window of time, actually relatively risk free.

When you are young, there is no *wrong* choice other than the safe choice.

And the safe choice usually isn't going anywhere.

Take two brothers, Bert and John Jacobs, straight out of school, broke, and seemingly lacking any direction, who bypassed the traditional path of résumé writing and job hunting and headed out across the country in a beat-up minivan, attempting to fund their trip by selling silk-screened T-shirts along the way. They didn't fare very well—in fact, you would say, at least from a monetary standpoint, they failed—until they came back to Cambridge, Massachusetts, with a new design. It was a simple graphic with a simple tagline that resonated with people: *Life is good.* I'm sure you have seen it on everything from T-shirts to Ultimate Discs to spare-tire covers. Their company, built around that single logo and graphic, is now estimated to be worth one hundred million dollars,[8] and, by their own accounts, life *is* good.

So how then, exactly, do you take a chance and invest in your own possibilities? Even if you acknowledge that the opportunity to drive across the country while supporting yourself by selling T-shirts from the trunk of your car (or whatever your own version of this might be) may not present itself as a viable option later in life, that it is likely a once-in-a-lifetime opportunity, how do you make it work? You may be

---

8. Seacoast Online, May 10, 2010, http://www.seacoastonline.com/articles/20100510-biz-5100302.

thinking to yourself that these endeavors don't all turn out the way we hope they will—that not every one of them will be a success. That most of them, in fact, will fail. And you would be right. After all, we don't hear about them when they don't succeed. Most times a half-baked idea

there are lots of people, a number of whom we are about to meet, who took relatively ordinary life experiences and responded to them in an extraordinary way, and it reaffirms an age-old notion.

The fires of greatness must be kindled with ordinary tinder.

And those great fires, often fueled by the twigs and broken branches of youth and the half-baked ideas of a risk-tolerant, one-hump, high-beta camel, can generate massive opportunity. They *can* be the foundation for one-hundred-million-dollar companies, like Life is good. And as I learned while interviewing people for this book, they can also help prevent malaria across Africa. They can educate and protect young women across the globe. They can help topple dictators, save Uganda's child soldiers, and give voices to the oppressed.

What can happen if an undergraduate agriculture major decides to take a risk by not heading back to manage the family ranch? Or what can happen if a film student gets on an airplane and heads to a war zone in search of a story with little more than a video camera? What can happen if we accept the premise that we can take a small risk by investing in ourselves?

What can happen is unbridled success.

∽

IN 1998, WHILE still an undergraduate animal science major at Texas A&M University, one of Elizabeth McKee's friends had to leave school when she had a baby because the university did not have a child-care program or facility that she could afford. Since Texas A&M is a big school with a large faculty and thousands of both undergraduate and graduate students, many of whom have families, Elizabeth was astonished that such a seemingly basic support system like child care was not available. She did some research and found out that Texas A&M was the only school in the Big 12 that didn't have a child-care facility, which surprised her even more. From there she tried to generate some interest in the issue on campus, then protested and caused a bit of a "ruckus," as she puts in, at which point the university president called her in and told her that if this was something she legitimately wanted to pursue, she needed to do so through student government.

After going through the necessary channels and getting her proposal approved by the student electorate, the university still didn't take action. "I went back to the president," Elizabeth tells me, "knocked on his door again, and he said, 'If you can raise the money,' which was three hundred twenty-five thousand dollars, I think, 'then we will give you the permission and the ability to build this facility at the school.'"

Elizabeth enlisted the support of a woman on campus named Mary Miller, who was a vice president of administration at the university at the time, and who had also expressed some interest in setting up a child-care facility. She told Elizabeth that if the students were behind it, she would help her raise the money. So they did.

"We raised the money," Elizabeth tells me matter-of-factly. "We built this amazing child-care facility on campus—I just about failed out of school. I was twenty and meeting with the construction crews and hiring people. And now, almost twelve years later, there are eleven languages spoken in this little children's center, and it absolutely turned me toward assessing a community problem and finding what finances are needed to help it, what administrative-type activities and approvals are needed, and how to keep it going—how to make it sustainable—

~~once was~~

~~.... way it was, and I~~ was happy with that," she says. "I didn't know that there was anything else out there, much less out of my town or even out of my state or out of the country."

So Elizabeth went back to Mary Miller, with whom she became close during their efforts to launch the child-care facility, explained her changed interest, and Mary told her that she should simply graduate with the degree she had been pursuing and consider raising money for the Texas A&M Foundation. "We have a great foundation here and you can learn about how it all works," she said, and Elizabeth took her advice. Then, while she was raising money for her alma mater, Elizabeth decided to take another risk—a trip on her own to Africa to, as she casually puts it, "Just check it out."

Elizabeth drove a truck across Namibia and into Angola, which was "a little crazy at the time," she tells me, smiling fondly. During this trip her eyes were opened to what was going on in the world on a humanitarian level. "I just had no idea. I got passionate about it and decided that I wanted to keep broadening my circle." Upon her return, she was inspired to start making moves in order to do just that—broaden her circle. "I did an internship on the Hill in Washington, D.C., and got a little bit of a fever for that, but learned I didn't want to be in politics, which was the best thing I've ever done in terms of learning what I do and don't believe in."

Now that she had an idea of what she wanted to do, Elizabeth worked during the day as a fund-raiser for her alma mater and began working on her graduate degree in nonprofit administration during the evenings. Not long after, she was approached with a new opportunity—a job offer from the Points of Light Foundation, an independent, non-partisan organization founded to encourage the engagement of public service based on former President George H. W. Bush's "Thousand Points of Light" inauguration speech—and she signed on to raise money. Elizabeth tells me that the role had nothing to do with Bush's politics; it was about her admiration and respect for the public service philosophy behind the foundation. "When they asked me to join the Points of Light Foundation, it was a pretty big deal to me, because it meant moving to Washington, D.C., and it meant making the 'I might never come back to the family ranch' decision, which was also a big deal. That meant no one else was going to take it on—it was a legacy thing." She moved to D.C. in January 2001, and while she was there she kept growing what she calls her "international passion."

It was at this point that Elizabeth made another key decision involving risk assessment. "I was at Points of Light, and made the decision that I should join the Peace Corps. I thought, 'If I'm serious about service and I'm serious about giving back long-term, what could be a better training ground or platform to do that?'"

While waiting for a response from the Peace Corps, she was offered a position at Share Our Strength, a "killer anti-hunger nonprofit," as she passionately describes it, to help run a campaign called the Great American Bake Sale. The premise, according to Elizabeth, was "How do you engage 'normal' people in thinking about hunger globally? Can people do bake sales in their own backyards but impact Ethiopia, or impact some other place?" The event was a massive success and created a movement that continues to this very day. (To give you an idea of just how big this cause is, I recently saw an advertisement for it on a bag of Domino sugar.)

Elizabeth had been with Share Our Strength for only about six months when she got the call from the Peace Corps. "Share Our Strength was absolutely wonderful and they asked me to stay, and the salary they put in front of me was pretty amazing, but I chose to go make two hundred dollars a month in Bolivia. So I took off to Bolivia.

...Elizabeth had limited electricity, no running water, and was bathing in the local river—but she loved it.

"The latrine fell in within about three months, so that was tricky," she laughs, "but I learned more in those two years and three months than I think I will probably sequentially learn for the rest of my life. What works, what doesn't. Traveling with other volunteers and looking at how development dollars are just dumped in some of these areas, and then people leave. Or you put a tractor somewhere thinking it will be used for farming, but then it's pulled apart for housing. Or, where I was, a German NGO[9] put a chicken farm there. The chickens kept pecking the women, so the locals buried them all and burned the place down because they thought it was evil," she tells me.

"I had these grand plans of changing the world and helping women and helping agriculture, but after about a year in, it was so apparent that these people knew everything they needed to know. They just needed our support. The right connections, a tiny bit of funding—but making sure they *led* all the ideas," Elizabeth emphasizes. "You had these indigenous people who had been there for ten generations, facing corrupt governments, or five years of drought—still they knew what

9. Nongovernmental organization.

they needed. If only someone could just come in and listen instead of *telling* them what they thought needed to happen."

In terms of her own career risk and altered trajectory, Elizabeth acknowledges where it all started. "My happy coincidence happened when I was in college, but the rest has been pure passion." As far as building a network and forging a career/life path that met her own standards? "You have to put all of these things into your tool chest and be able to pull them out five years later," she says, as she shows me pictures of her diverse travels. "It's also really, really okay to be the youngest person in the room. There is a huge value in that. If you have the respect of someone sitting across from you, and you don't try to be as old as them, or as smart as them, and you say, 'You are my mentor and I am going to learn from *everything* you have to offer, and respect that, and give them that deference, then you are a lucky person. I was the youngest and the first female fund-raiser at the Texas A&M Foundation, and when I went in, I remember I was trying to look all buttoned-up in my gray suit, and trying to look older and act older, and trying to know what I was talking about, which I didn't. And I started to think, 'These people *do* have thirty years' more experience—learn from it, listen, treat that with great respect.' I have placed one hundred percent value in every person I have met along the way, and respected their advice. When I was at Points of Light, I got to meet every living president," she tells me. "I mean, that's crazy. But I also got to meet heads of small-town volunteer centers, who I think are just as global, just as smart, and I learned from what they were doing."

Elizabeth's first low-risk, high-reward scenario came when she decided to invest herself in something she believed in, and campaigned to build a child-care facility at her school. This was an ordinary experience that she responded to in an extraordinary way. In so doing, but without any intent to do so, she discovered something that she both loved and was good at. By not returning to her family's ranch as originally planned, she took a more personal risk. But the ranch wasn't going anywhere—at least for the short term. If she decided to, Elizabeth still had the option to reassess her situation and revert to her original plan. Nothing she had done up until that point had changed anything permanently. Arguably, her most significant risk was taken when she left a

And that proved to be the case, and then some.

Elizabeth McKee Gore is now the Executive Director of Global Partnerships for the United Nations Foundation, the international institution founded by renowned entrepreneur and philanthropist Ted Turner to "foster partnerships that strengthen the UN and support its causes."[10] She has spearheaded and overseen several world-changing initiatives, including the Nothing But Nets campaign (you may be aware of the television commercials, the feature in *Sports Illustrated* by Rick Reilly, or their partnership with the NBA), which has raised thirty-three million dollars and distributed over three million mosquito nets with the goal of eliminating malaria-related deaths in Africa by 2015.[11]

Her other responsibilities include managing and branding multi-million-dollar partnerships with the Bill & Melinda Gates Foundation, a campaign in excess of one hundred million dollars with the Global Fund, and her newest endeavor, Girl Up, which, among other objectives, serves to empower and educate young women who are facing child marriages, lack of education, and premature death in communities around the world. In short, she is one of the major players on the world's philanthropic stage

10. The United Nations Foundation.
11. Nothing But Nets 2009 Annual Report.

and is responsible for facilitating life-saving initiatives on a daily basis. In recognition of her accomplishments, in 2008 Elizabeth was named as one of the Top 100 Extraordinary Women in the world by *People* magazine.

And she thought all she knew how
to do was to take care of cows.

As we sat in Elizabeth's downtown Washington, D.C., office, I was struck by the fact that her walls were not adorned with the traditional college diplomas, awards, accolades, newspaper clippings, and certificates of achievement that one might expect to find surrounding someone of her stature. Instead, I saw pictures and mementos from her life as a global citizen—photos of the small hut she inhabited while living in Bolivia, a picture of her with a group of her friends at the summit of Mount Kilimanjaro, and some small gifts and tokens of remembrance that she has collected. Looking around her office and spending a few hours in conversation, it became clear that Elizabeth McKee Gore got to where she is today by recognizing that she could take a few calculated risks and invest in her own possibilities. And like the universal truth that seems to define success, her success began with an extraordinary response to relatively ordinary events.

She was able to assess the risk-reward at each
career juncture with spot-on accuracy.

Elizabeth's story not only demonstrates how relatively ordinary experiences can lead to extraordinary success if we don't allow perceived barriers to restrict us, but it also speaks to the importance of reassessing our own opportunity cost.

Taking small risks when we have very little to lose and
everything to gain is a critical catalyst for success.

⌇

JASON RUSSELL, FRESH out of college, along with his friends, freshman Laren Poole and sophomore Bobby Bailey, were aspiring film—

..., Uganda was engulfed in a brutally violent civil war that "we knew nothing about," Jason tells me. The theocratic campaign led by Joseph Kony of the Lord's Resistance Army (LRA) had claimed the lives of over thirty thousand children and displaced nearly two million Ugandan citizens. Children were routinely kidnapped from their families and forced to fight hand to hand as foot soldiers on the front lines of this war. It is estimated that between sixty thousand to more than a hundred thousand Ugandan children have suffered such a fate and that 90 percent of Kony's soldiers were abducted as children.[12] The world community hadn't done anything to successfully stop it, and when these three travelers witnessed this humanitarian crisis firsthand, they decided to try to do something about it themselves.

As much as they became enraged at the systemic holocaust occurring before their very eyes, Jason, Laren, and Bobby also became inspired. Unnecessary, unjustifiable death was happening all around them, and once on the ground, they captured it on film. The three of them returned home, edited and released their film as a documentary called *Invisible Children: Rough Cut,* and launched a nonprofit organization in 2005 appropriately called Invisible Children. Their goal was to bring attention to the atrocities that were happening under the reign of Joseph Kony and to

12. http://www.WorldVision.org.

force lawmakers to remove this war criminal from power in order to help bring an end to a civil war that had been ongoing for the past two decades.

Invisible Children quickly became a full-time endeavor. The story and message went viral, with people joining the online movement, requesting screenings of the film, and offering assistance in whatever way they could. The Invisible Children project grew as an international cause and eventually began attracting millions of dollars in funding,[13] as well as attention from lawmakers and politicians in the United States— all generated by a massive online presence, hundreds of full-time volunteers, and tens of thousands of supporters from around the world.

One of the organization's big moments came after they were already fairly sizable in terms of their network, when they harnessed the power of relationships to win the million-dollar prize for a fund-raising competition held by Chase Bank. "We made something like fifty thousand phone calls," Jason tells me. "We were pulling our hair out. We didn't sleep. By personally contacting people we were able to win the competition in the final seconds." Invisible Children was giving out hundreds of scholarships to Ugandan students each year, supporting recovering child soldiers, and running strategic marketing campaigns to raise both awareness and money for the people they wanted so desperately to help. Pretty impressive results, considering that the organization's founders were undergraduate students just a few years earlier.

And they were just getting started.

"We don't want to wait on bureaucracy," Jason tells me. After a few years of networking, both digitally and face-to-face, the Invisible Children team began the process of gathering signatures on a petition to convince Congress and the president of the United States to issue a citizen's arrest warrant for Joseph Kony, since charges of war crimes had

---

13. Invisible Children Independent Audit Report, 2009.

failed to stick on more than one occasion. The result of their efforts was nothing short of astounding—over 250,000 signatures on the citizen's arrest warrant, a Washington, D.C., demonstration that became the largest African-issue lobby day in U.S. history, and an eleven-day cam-

[text obscured by scanning artifact]

..........g for government intervention to remove Joseph Kony from power and save the lives of *thousands* of children—children who are or would become victims of Kony and his militia. Jason, Laren, and Invisible Children CEO Ben Keesey were in the Oval Office with the president when he signed the bill into law. President Obama shook their hands, and he commented on a story they had told him about a child soldier named Jacob, whom they met when they were in Uganda, by saying, as Jason paraphrases, "If you ever meet that boy again, tell him that the president of the United States is going to do something about this issue."

No one would disagree that these three students took on personal risk by traveling to a region involved in a brutal, decades-old civil war. But what they *didn't* do was take a career risk. What they created for themselves when they flew to Sudan, from a life and career standpoint, was unbridled opportunity. No one *expected* them to produce an award-winning documentary, and certainly nobody could ever have predicted that they would build a multi-million-dollar humanitarian organization or spur a grass-

14. http://www.InvisibleChildren.com.

15. On March 5, 2012, Invisible Children released a thirty-minute documentary film called KONY 2012 that became the most viral video in history (as reported by Visible Measures), receiving 112 million views in six days. This film was part of a campaign to direct global attention to the crisis in order to stop Joseph Kony and end the killings.

roots movement that would bring to the floor of the United States Congress a bill that would be signed into law. And nobody expected that they would have, as Jason tells me, "over one hundred people on the ground in Uganda, ensuring that action is taking place," or be responsible for saving the lives of what may very well be thousands of children halfway around the world.

They were just headed out in their
version of a beat-up minivan.

〜

EVERY TIME I spoke with successful individuals about how they started out, even if where they ended up was decades and miles from where they began, I was told, in essence, the same story—that story of heading out across the desert with some half-baked idea looking for tinder to build a great fire. They all recounted tales of what amounted to taking a relatively risk-free "risk," and it always, at least indirectly, is what led them to where they are today. In one way or another, all of these successful people took a look at their situation and decided that they had nowhere to go but up, and that sent them on a journey. And every one of those journeys turned out to be a success catalyst. Even if these journeys fell short of extraordinary, even if they seemingly failed, they paved the way toward other potential opportunities down the road.

Elizabeth McKee Gore's life changed when she made the decision to take on the challenge of raising funds to build a child-care facility at Texas A&M. Jason Russell, Laren Poole, and Bobby Bailey's lives changed when they flew to Sudan with a video camera. We will see in the chapters that follow that this is a pattern that is repeated over and again with virtually all of the people that I interviewed.

These successful people all responded in an extraordinary
way to relatively ordinary events, and they all took
on a relatively risk-free "risk."

Yet even though these may have *felt* like random decisions to them at the time, and they might seem like random events when we read about them now, these young people made decisions to respond to very *specific* opportunities. These were not random decisions at all. In fact, Elizabeth

She chose this specific opportunity because she knew something about herself. And she succeeded because she listened to her gut.

In the book *How We Decide,* author Jonah Lehrer cites a study by Ap Dijksterhuis of the University of Amsterdam. First published in the journal *Science*, Dijksterhuis's study explains that the human brain can only process a certain amount of information before it becomes overloaded and relegates the decision-making process to the unconscious mind.

Dijksterhuis's study shows that when there is too much information to process, we actually make better decisions; we make the *right* choice with a higher frequency when we go with our gut instincts. Essentially, what he found is that in complex decision making, in situations where we cannot possibly process all of the information in an *analytical* way, we are led to the right choice when we allow our unconscious minds to make the decision for us.[16] Dijksterhuis uses the example of the relatively complex decision-making process involved in choosing which car to buy. Since most people can't process all of the technical car facts in a way that will make sense, they end up buying the "right car" for

16. Greg Miller, "Tough Decision? Don't Sweat It," *Science*, February 17, 2006.

themselves after listening to all of the information about different cars and then going with their gut.

Our broad life decisions are far more complex and encumbered with a greater number of overwhelming, unpredictable variables than those involved in buying a new car, and the consequences are certainly more far-reaching. Yet in explaining how consumers are led to buy the right car, Dijksterhuis is also explaining why Elizabeth McKee Gore chose to raise money for the child-care facility and why Jason, Laren, and Bobby got on that plane for Sudan. In essence, he is explaining why we should allow young people to head out across the desert in a beat-up minivan of their own choosing.

> *Our choices in these matters are not random*
> *at all. But we do have to make sure that we*
> *don't let the right opportunities slip by.*

If we acknowledge that, with relatively few commitments, young people are "gifted" a uniquely low-risk window of time to invest in themselves, we have to first make sure that we recognize these opportunities when they present themselves to us, and then we need to assess the risk-reward ratio correctly and act accordingly. By not selling ourselves short when we are young, by assessing our risk and recognizing that when we have nothing to lose and potentially everything to gain, we can create extraordinary opportunities that alter our perspective and, in turn, our life trajectory.

> *These experiences, when they result in success, can have*
> *profound personal, financial, social, and even political*
> *results. But even if they fail, even if they do not take*
> *us where we want to go, they provide the life fodder*
> *that directs and even helps define us as we navigate*
> *our way toward that next opportunity.*

3

New-School Capitalism, Containment Booms,
Symbolic Superheroes, and Very Important Carrots

■

> Take away my people, but leave my factories, and
> soon grass will grow on the factory floors. Take
> away my factories, but leave my people, and soon
> we will have a new and better factory.
>
> —ANDREW CARNEGIE

WHEN I FIRST set out to interview people for this book, I thought it would be interesting to take note of what *they* wanted to talk about. I certainly knew what I wanted to ask them, but by their agreeing to be interviewed I knew that each of them had something they wanted me to know about their companies, organizations, or life stories. After doing meticulous research, and entering each conversation with a list of my own questions, in each case I paid careful attention to what the interviewee felt compelled to talk about—figuring that whatever constructs were top of mind for them should probably also be top of mind for me.

When I interviewed Michael "Mickey" McManus, the president and CEO of MAYA Design, Inc., a high-concept design firm and think tank that finds solutions to complex issues, ranging from the future of digital storage to land-mine detection, he was more excited to talk about filling an office with plastic balls and building superhero replicas of MAYA's best employees than discussing the latest mind-bending research they were conducting for DARPA (Defense Advanced Research Projects Agency). While we covered many diverse topics and complex innovative concepts over the course of our conversation, and Mickey was more than happy to answer my questions, what he *wanted* to tell me about were stories focused on MAYA's company culture and how these stories reflected their core business model and management approach. From the perspective of the CEO, more so than sales and marketing statistics, superheroes and plastic balls were the demonstrative elements of MAYA's company ethos.

Similarly, when I spent a day with Ido Leffler of Yes To, Inc., which is one of the fastest-growing natural beauty brands in America, he was more inclined to talk about his Very Important Carrots (Yes To's best customers who have his personal cell phone number) and the Yes To Seed Fund (which helps inner-city schools and communities plant gardens) than he was to boast about their rapid-fire financial growth or new-product development. He proudly introduced me to both executives and interns and invited me to sit in on employee meetings, despite my being an "outsider."

Neither one of these corporate leaders felt particularly compelled to relay how much money their respective companies generate or what share of the market they control. They were fabulous interviewees on every level—forthcoming and available, answering all of my questions directly—but it was clear that what both of them *wanted* to talk about was their company culture. And for good reason.

They had created company cultures that uniquely define
not only their respective businesses but, in turn,
themselves and their employees as well.

...........the daily culture at Its 10, I could tell within five minutes of visiting the office that I would love to work there as well, despite never having once considered entering the field of health and beauty, cosmetics, or consumer packaged goods. In fact, I became so excited about both of these companies that I quickly realized that we are often so consumed with simply getting *a* job that we forget to make sure we get the *right* job at the *right* company.

The reason I was being told about plastic balls and superheroes and Very Important Carrots and Seed Funds is because *culture* is hard to explain in concrete terms—in most cases, it's something you have to experience. Try for example, off the top of your head, to differentiate between the personalities of two well-known colleges or even two foreign countries, in definitive terms. One could say that one school is more "preppy" than another, or fosters closer faculty-student relationships due to smaller class size, or that different languages are spoken in two European countries, or that the food is different, or perhaps point to lifestyle or political differences, but it is very hard to capture in conversation the intangible nuances of culture.

In applying this reasoning to the study of corporate culture, I realized *why* I was being told these stories, but I wanted to understand the motivation *behind* this high-level focus on positive company culture and the climate at these organizations. After all, creating a fun, positive, and supportive work environment or an altruistic agenda does not, on the surface, make much economic sense. In fact, while it is great for employees, it sounds expensive; and these are *for-profit* companies. What I observed, however, is that culture can supersede and transcend traditional corporate strategies and often function to build even larger profit.

And that got me thinking about
capitalism in a whole new way.

⌒

NO ONE WOULD disagree with the premise that capitalism is as much a social system as it is an economic one. It represents not only a way of producing and distributing goods, but a way of thinking and living as well. At its core, it is a system designed to benefit the individual—the capitalist—who is looking to profit: to market a product, service, or skill for his or her own financial gain.

This is a simplistic view, however; a sterile, textbook model of what is a dynamic system affected by countless variables. A free market economy left in pure theoretical form would mimic Charles Darwin's model for natural selection and survival of the fittest. It would, in fact, evolve companies with cultures that mandate "profit at any cost." And it certainly has. But capitalism, of course, does not operate on the pages of an economics book. It operates in the human marketplace. And the human marketplace, behavioral and social scientists have shown us time and again, is regulated by more than just the bottom line. There are factors and variables, including work environment and the desire to be altruistic, that impact economies and jobs and don't exist in either free market economic theory or on Darwin's Galápagos Islands.

Generally speaking, human beings have a strong desire to behave in a morally good way—to actually help others. And that runs counter to both Darwin's theory of survival of the fittest and the philosophy of the old-school companies where, for both the finch and the financier, "the sharpest (not the kindest) beak should prevail."[17]

Creating a positive work environment and a socially conscious corporate structure has never been an integral part of the pure capitalist

expensive, and companies only do it when they have to. Any positive company culture was often mere "window dressing"—part of a public relations campaign used to build brand image, or part of a compensation package needed to attract the best-qualified employees.

Yet what I saw and heard when I spoke with many corporate leaders is that just like one of the highly studied species from the Galápagos Islands, capitalism is evolving. And it is doing so in a way that would have made even Charles Darwin pause. This is the era of *I want it now, I want it better, and I want it differently.* And as such, it has produced a new class of entrepreneurs, leaders, and CEOs who are moving toward *self*-regulation. It could be said that in their hands, capitalism and corporate responsibility have met head-on, and where we see this best reflected is in their respective company cultures. These select companies, the majority of which are *for-profit*, are, in varying degrees, inherently altruistic, and in some very special cases even almost poetically symbiotic, as they change what we expect from our jobs and what we as consumers expect from the products we purchase and the corporations that we buy them from.

As a result, they are great places to work.

17. Charles Darwin, *Autobiography.*

Unlike old-school, profit-at-any-cost companies, these new leaders have created a corporate climate that keeps people happy. They offer not only their employees, but also the consumers and clients who buy their products or services, a genuine sense of worth and personal satisfaction. They operate in an environment that is respectful to the world around them *and* they produce a profit. They respect the journey and the road on which they are traveling, not just the destination.

Luckily for us, as Darwin observed, natural selection prevails. "Favorable variations would tend to be preserved, and unfavorable ones to be destroyed."[18] Which means quite simply that these companies, modeled upon a new derivative of capitalism, are here to stay. Companies that combine profit with a culturally dynamic, employee-friendly environment and a social conscience are simply, in the parlance of this new century, not "too *big* to fail," but rather, too *good* to fail.

But just as I was in the midst of setting up interviews and immersed in speaking with corporate leaders about their respective company cultures and thinking that there was a significant trend in the corporate world that had many companies evolving in an interesting and positive way, we were hit with news of a catastrophic oil spill in the Gulf of Mexico.

〜

ON APRIL 20, 2010, an explosion inside an underwater drilling rig called the Deepwater Horizon, which was owned and operated by British Petroleum (BP), caused the largest ecological disaster to date in North American history. What resulted was a catastrophic environmental event in the Gulf of Mexico, with oil spilling into the waters off the Louisiana coast at a staggering rate. As months went by, the spill loomed unstoppable as hundreds of millions of gallons of crude oil continued to gush into the once pristine waters of the Gulf, not only

18. Charles Darwin, *The Origin of Species.*

devastating the environment in immeasurable ways but also fundamentally destroying segments of the local economy for years and, quite
possibly, decades to come. Even by the most optimistic standards, the
damage to both marine life and human livelihoods was deemed to be

tive. Despite decades of record earnings, the oil companies simply had
no motivation to invest the capital necessary to develop the technology to
deal with a spill of this magnitude. The government didn't mandate that
they do so, and the companies themselves felt no sense of responsibility—
social, moral, or otherwise—to develop cleanup measures of their own
accord. As oil poured into the Gulf, chemical dispersants and simple
containment booms—low-tech metal-and-foam barriers that float on
the water's surface to help block the spread of the oil—were offered as a
paltry best bet.

Not long after, and on the very same day that the U.S. Coast Guard
announced that emulsified oil in the form of tar balls had begun wash-
ing up on the Louisiana coast, executives from BP, Transocean, and
Halliburton (BP's drilling partners) sat in Senate hearings pointing fin-
gers at one another in an attempt to limit their corporate responsibility
and financial losses.

That same week (mid-May 2010) in Washington, D.C., and just a few
miles away from those Senate hearings, I sat in the audience listening to
former president Bill Clinton address a small group of young entrepreneurs, ideators, and philanthropists who had a radically different mind-set

19. Steven Mufson, "Oil Cleanup Technology Hasn't Kept Pace," *Washington Post*,
May 4, 2010.

from that of those oil industry executives. Rather than finger-pointing, this group of thought leaders had come together to openly and willingly take responsibility for their companies, for the environment in which they live and work, and to embrace the opportunity they have to participate in positive, fundamental social and global change.

"Our problems relate to rigidity," stated Clinton, emphasizing the need to break through older-generation corporate, governmental, and social barriers in order to address the biggest challenges facing the modern world. "Institutions tend to become fossilized," he said, adding that "breaking through is not enough."

Clinton discussed the rapid rise of companies utilizing socially conscious business solutions to solve humanitarian issues, stating that of the over 1 million NGOs and roughly 350,000 community and religious organizations doing philanthropic work around the world, more than half were initiated since the mid-1990s. Clinton declared that "we need to put America back in the tomorrow business," a sentiment that was received with nods of agreement and applause from the audience of mostly twenty- and thirty-somethings, who to a large degree exemplified a tangible shift in generational expectations and values.

"You have more tomorrows than yesterdays," Clinton closed, encouraging the young game changers in the audience to continue to do their part as they collectively reinvent the landscape for business, as well as for philanthropy and social action, in the years to come. "Now we have to get out there and break down these barriers before it's too late."

As Clinton was ending his speech, oil continued to flow off the coast of Louisiana at an unprecedented rate into the now devastated Gulf of Mexico, as it would continue to spill, uncontained, for months to come. And as I sat in the audience, thinking that perhaps the executives from BP, Transocean, and Halliburton should have stopped by for a listen, I realized that it would have been a pointless endeavor because they could never understand the fundamental difference between "them" and "us," between the old-school, fossilized businesses that President

Clinton referenced and the new breed of entrepreneurs seated in the audience that evening.

These new-school entrepreneurs and business leaders

...... a company's DNA, seeded in the corporate mind-set and business model from conception, it changes everything from the success trajectory and the bottom line to the dynamics of the workplace that each of these companies provides for its employees. Unlike the executives from BP and so many others, these new leaders are not running their companies for profit at any cost.

Their focus is on "profit with purpose."

The difference between the fossils of business and the future of business is fundamentally that these new leaders believe that the *way* in which they earn that profit actually matters. It follows rather naturally then that when the route to profit, and not just the profit itself, matters, the structure, culture, and mind-set at the company fundamentally changes as well.

So the important question becomes, How are these new companies and leaders moving away from "old-school" and creating "new-school" in terms of construct, action, and culture? In speaking with some of these leaders, one thing became very clear. These companies are constructed *differently* from the ground up. Profit and good, both journey and destination, are unmistakably intertwined.

And the "good" is metastasizing in profound ways.

It is good for the employees; it is good for the customers who buy the products or services; it is good for the community; and as counterintuitive as it might seem, it is good for the bottom line. The "good" is embedded in the structure, the culture, the employment practices, and in the philosophical agenda of these enterprises. We are in a softer, kinder era of business leaders, and the reason this should be important to all of us is that these are the types of companies that we should *want* to work for.

Because "good" will never need containment booms.

⤿

MICKEY MCMANUS IS currently the president and CEO of MAYA[20] Design, Inc., a Pittsburgh-based company that utilizes innovative techniques, combining technology and information, to create user-friendly experiences. The MAYANS, which is how they refer to their family of practitioners, have an impressive portfolio of clients and projects, including design and research work for Samsung, Merrill Lynch, GE Energy, the USPS, Whirlpool, Target, and Hewlett-Packard, among many more.[21]

In addition, and perhaps more importantly, MAYA is consistently ranked among the top small businesses to work for in the country. In 2009, the Great Place to Work Institute, Inc. and the Society for Human Resource Management ranked MAYA as one of the top twenty-five small companies to work for in America. The 2010 Great Place to Work Rankings presented by *Entrepreneur*, ranked MAYA as one of the top twenty-five small workplaces. Also in 2010, *Inc.* magazine and Winning Workplaces recognized MAYA as one of twenty Top Small Company Workplaces winners.

20. MAYA is an acronym for Most Advanced, Yet Acceptable.
21. http://www.MAYA.com.

"We share twenty percent of our profits each quarter with *everyone* at the company," says Mickey, and I can feel the sense of pride in his voice as he shares this fact. He's simply that excited about MAYA's culture. "We're flat.[22] Everyone in our company sees our books each quar-

...., ... invests in the business ideas of *their own employees*. On more than one occasion, with MAYA's support, these "side projects" have turned into multi-million-dollar companies.

"People get a chance to explore," Mickey tells me, "we grow by cell division." MAYA also engages its team in social activities, including "common reads," in which everyone at the company reads the same book, then discusses it on a day when the office is closed for this specific purpose. And this isn't business homework in disguise. "These are often history books or stories about amazing people or adventures, because we don't think any of us learn enough from history, and to look forward, we think you have to look back even further," Mickey explains. Another aspect of their culture? Senior leaders, Mickey included, design and build superhero action figures (by surgically altering plastic toys and figurines) that represent the traits and characteristics of excelling employees and present them as awards of achievement. It shows they care about their team.

"I think it's important," Mickey says. "I'll literally be in a room making a twelve-inch action figure for one of our best young employees, piecing together different items and objects from other action figures to

22. "Flat" is a corporate term that refers to the intentional lack of traditional hierarchy within an institution.

capture the essence of the recipient, trying not to cut off my thumb." Remember, this is coming from the CEO and president of a highly successful company with millions of dollars in annual revenue. Why would he spend his assumably valuable time on seemingly silly projects?

Because great company culture revolves around a
positive focus on employees and flat leadership.

MAYA hires and works with everyone from technology and design experts to anthropologists and cognitive psychologists—there are very few limits in terms of the *type* of person they are looking for when adding to their team. This isn't to say they'll hire just anyone—you need to be smart, to be sure—but there is no archetypical employee or team member. "We have an animator from DreamWorks sitting next to someone who taught English in Japan, across from a lead vocalist in a rock band who happens to also be a senior human scientist. Down the hall there is a bricks-and-mortar architect next to an industrial designer, cognitive psychologist, and computer scientist," Mickey tells me. They also regularly promote from within—including interns. "One kid we brought in as an intern during college received two job offers when he graduated. He had an offer from MAYA, and he had an offer from Apple." It is a testament to the company culture that he stayed with MAYA.

Shortly after taking over as the president of MAYA in 2001, Mickey decided that he wanted to get a better understanding of how many people were sending e-mails to his team each week. He found out that the number of e-mails, on average, was just over ten thousand, but he felt that it was a difficult number to tangibly quantify, so he decided to do something dramatic. Mickey ordered one plastic ball for every e-mail the company was receiving each week. These are the same plastic balls that are typically found in play pits for children at places like McDonald's—the ones that kids dive into and roll around in after going down the slide. They're not cheap, and certainly not easy to store—especially when there

are so many of them. And collecting them was a brazen move for someone who had just taken over the role of company president, one might
think.

Mickey went into the MAYA offices that weekend, sawed the door

as a result, defines who they are as a company—only a company with a
unique, flexible culture could actually find a way to incorporate this
"stunt" into their daily operations.

Not long after the room was filled with those plastic balls, some
potential strategic clients were visiting the office—the office of a leading
design firm that for some reason had thousands of plastic balls filling
up one of their most visible work spaces—for a meeting about a possible
"global project." Upon seeing the half-door and the immense pit of
what were essentially silly children's toys, rather than bolting for the
exits, one of the potential clients immediately "kicked off his shoes,
opened the half-door, and dove headfirst into the pit of balls," recounts
Mickey. "Are we going to be having the meeting in here?" the visitor
asked, as he rolled around in the pit, smiling and laughing. "It was right
then that I knew that these were clients we wanted to work with,"
Mickey says. "They got it."

The room full of plastic balls ended up becoming a mainstay at the
MAYA offices for several years, until they relocated. The original idea,
which was simply meant as an exercise to help quantify the "growing
amount of information we have to slog through each day," became
symbolic of something much larger and more important—MAYA's culture. "We continued to use that room as a litmus test," says Mickey. "If
you 'got' the fun and deep meaning of the balls, then you understood

how we work, how we think, and frankly, we want to be in a space with people who get it."

In speaking with Mickey, it is clear that every aspect of MAYA's culture is designed to nurture the employees. And for good reason. Especially when working in the field of "Big Ideas."

Dissatisfaction at work derails innovation.[23]
And innovation leads to bigger profits.

"We're focused on what nature can teach us about computing systems, sort of biomimicry for the information age," Mickey explains to me. "Nature has survived some pretty tough challenges and is incredibly resilient. We'd like to view our task as protecting the world's information for the future. That's what makes people come in every morning," says Mickey. He then refers to what he calls "brittleness" when it comes to business, design, data storage, and analytical problem solving. "Five years ago, you would find that most companies (who you use to store your most important data, personal information, and images) had their own teams of employees and methods of storage. Now, they have gotten rid of data and smart people and put all of their eggs into roughly five massive clouds, or baskets."

So what happens when one of those networks goes down and loses your information? "You have to rebuild *everything* you ever did," emphasizes Mickey, in reference to the very realistic possibility that we may be entering what he calls a "shoe-box dark age" when it comes to the world's information storage, warning us that any digital content that we have saved anywhere will likely be lost forever unless we find a better way of storing it. "The shoe-box dark age symbolizes the fact that generations of us have stored our family pictures, wedding certificates, and old movies in shoe boxes, which, while not great, could last genera-

23. http://www.cbsnews.com/stories/2010/01/05/national/main6056611.shtml.

tions in the basement," Mickey explains. "Now there is a generation that has never printed out and saved memories, who expect the magical cloud to do it for them. We're centralizing things that should never be centralized."

― ―ge ――.― pu.―..―, ―――u u―――――ei, ―viickey ―ells me. The reason that Mickey and his team at MAYA are so forward-thinking is that they *didn't* get rid of the data and smart people, as many other companies began to do with the exponential growth of technology and the increased ease of outsourcing and automating. Instead, they continue to *gather* data and *retain* smart people to try to prevent problems before they occur.

"I'm passionate," says Mickey. "We're a group of fellow travelers, and we're going somewhere. Whole industries are going to be popping up overnight while others will disappear." MAYA's role, and Mickey's job, is to make sure they remain on the cutting edge, and their employees are nurtured to think that way. "How are we going to prevent another 9/11?" asks Mickey. It's no wonder that DARPA, a government organization that funded the research for what would become the Internet way back in 1969, has funded MAYA with millions of dollars to basically predict the future. Currently, MAYA is working on developing technology to better locate roadside bombs.

Several months after we spoke, Mickey followed up with me in regard to the status of this project. "Via DARPA, our team was working with the military to build a new kind of collaborative decision-making system that could radically reduce the time it takes to understand complex battlefield situations (like if roadside bombs exist somewhere) and dramatically increase the ability for teams to make better decisions about that information. It has since been deployed and saved countless lives. The system is called the "Command Post of the Future," he told me.

In speaking with leaders like Mickey, it is clear that they are not simply building a means to a profit end. Rather, they are running companies with a socially conscious agenda and building a like-minded workforce along the way. Of course, one might argue that since MAYA Design manufactures "Big Ideas," it makes perfect sense that they might be wired differently than other companies. In a way it is apropos: given that what MAYA does is so forward-thinking, the plastic balls and superhero action figures actually fit the culture perfectly. An exception to the rule, perhaps? Yet it became very clear when I visited other businesses that this approach to profit, one routed through positive corporate culture, employee satisfaction, and a broad sense of global responsibility, works regardless of the industry or what is being manufactured or sold.

↬

YES TO, INC. is a natural beauty and cosmetics company that was cofounded by Ido Leffler, who was born in Israel, raised in Australia, and has more than just profit on his mind. Yes To uses high-quality organic fruits and vegetables to create creams, lotions, and hair-care products for men, women, and children at an affordable price. What Ido Leffler and Lance Kalish, his businesses partner, cofounder, and self-described "numbers guy," have accomplished in just a few years is nothing short of astounding. The initial run was called Yes To Carrots, which features beta-carotene and minerals from the Dead Sea (highly desirable derivatives that not only make your skin look and feel better but also healthier). After rapid success, the company expanded to include Yes To Cucumbers, Yes To Tomatoes, Yes To Blueberries, and even a line of baby products called Yes To Baby Carrots.

Aside from being nearly 100 percent natural and consumer-driven, Yes To created a 501(c)3 nonprofit upon launching called the Yes To

Seed Fund, which provides funding, seeds (literally), and opportunities for education and knowledge pertaining to sustainable agriculture for young students and at-risk youth. A portion of every single sale of their products, whether it is lip balm, facial cream, shampoo, or otherwise,

America and what is the second largest mass-market natural beauty brand in the United States. Considering that Yes To was founded in Israel in 2006, opened its first U.S. office in 2007, and set up headquarters in San Francisco at the end of 2008, and that Ido didn't even move to the States until 2009, their fast-paced growth is nothing short of remarkable. By 2010, Yes To had been featured in the *New York Times, People, Cosmopolitan, Elle, InStyle, Seventeen, O, Glamour,* and *Good Housekeeping* and been seen on *Today,* the *Martha Stewart Show, The View,* and CNN.

Yet Ido is more excited to talk about the recent grant they gave to an elementary school that will provide funding for a community garden, educate children in both agriculture and nutrition, and even teach them about business as the harvested vegetables and fruits are then sold at the local farmers' market. "It's amazing, but a lot of kids think that tomatoes come from a can," says Ido. "They've never been exposed to basic facts that many of us take for granted. Even just seeing a tomato growing on a vine can be a life-altering experience, one that can affect not only the children but also their parents." Ido then jumps into a passionate description of the work they are doing with the Three Sisters Program in Ohio, which buys land to build sustainable gardens that support not only the local Native American culture but also the community of Somalian families, who miss the food and culture from back home, and battered local women, for whom the garden provides the opportunity for a "nurturing experience," as he puts it.

In the purest sense, Yes To is a prime example of a brand that has built a positive company culture by integrating a sense of social consciousness into the fabric of who they are. Upon visiting their offices I was particularly struck by how imbedded this culture actually is. It's evident in everything from the design of the headquarters—the furniture and carpets match the colors of their packaged products—to employees showing up early by choice on a Monday, to the core ideas behind their day-to-day operations.

"The word *no* was never an option for us," Ido tells me, taking a sip from a carrot-flavored Odwalla drink inside his company's conference room, which is adorned with the latest Yes To products and paintings of vegetables, a flat-screen TV, a Nintendo Wii, and even a classic foosball table for employees who need to "let the stress out." (Just to demonstrate how important workplace culture is to him, Ido e-mailed me months later, writing, "Wait until you see the new office with table tennis.") The hallways are carpeted in bright carrot-orange, the instructions printed on the shampoo bottles suggest that you "apply to wet hair while singing," and these are just a couple of the markers that suggest that Yes To is more than a brand; it is a way of thinking.

Differently.

"There were some great natural and organic cosmetics out there, but there was nothing you could feel emotionally vested in," Ido tells me. "I read somewhere that by the age of two, the average child has heard the word *no* two thousand times. So we decided to be all about *yes*."

∽

IT'S EVIDENT THAT Leffler and his leadership team recognize the value of being inclusive. Reiterating what Mickey from MAYA Design and so many others told me, Ido states, "Our leadership is flat, with everyone involved in practically everything. We have a culture where people just *do it.*" The company is so transparent and inclusive, in fact, that I was invited to sit in on a meeting with new employees. Unlike

more than happy to travel over one hundred days each year, away from her family, considering that she doesn't particularly *need* to do so, her answer is simple. "One word," she says smiling. "Potential." The passion and energy in the air was nothing short of inspiring—from the mantra of saying yes to the power and importance of close relationships with their best customers (aka Very Important Carrots), from how they treat their employees to the array of new natural products they are developing.

A key factor in Yes To's growth is clearly the people behind it. That said, the key to the success of the people behind the company is the *culture* its leaders create. Yes To promotes from within. They offer tuition reimbursement for employees and college credit for interns—things that on the surface are available at a lot of companies. But the cultural advantage at Yes To goes far beyond the standard corporate "competitive" benefits package. This philosophy of good permeates and defines them—it isn't window dressing or an addendum to company policy— and it has been this way since the very moment Ido and his partner started the business.

"We don't like to employ people, we like to *adopt* people," says Ido. "How can we add to the weirdness, the quirkiness of our company? People here will do anything for the company because they believe in it."

Ido goes on to tell me, quite enthusiastically, that despite the Yes To brand being carried in over thirty thousand stores in twenty-one coun-tries and growing by the day, he has conference calls every quarter with the Very Important Carrots. "They feel like they are part of the decision-making process, and we appreciate their opinions and ideas. We value their feedback," he explains.

"Just recently, one of our favorite interns showed up for her last day. She officially graduated college the day before, and she was getting ready to go off into the 'real' world. Instead, we offered her a full-time position the next day," says Ido, as it becomes even more evident that Yes To is like a large family.

In terms of hiring new employees, regardless of expertise or knowl-edge area, Ido and his team tend to look for certain personality types—outgoing, forward-thinking, and, most important, positive. "We're not particularly interested in helping people build their résumé," he tells me rather frankly, noting that many of the applications they receive are those of people who have been jumping from job to job once every two years or so. "If you have been bouncing around, explain *why* in your cover letter," he says, reinforcing the value of the cover letter as the first line of communication job seekers often have with potential employers. "We believe in our people. We throw them into the deep end and give them complete trust from the get-go," says Ido, whose statement is later exemplified by an undergraduate summer intern from Boston College named Lauren Matthews.

"Most of my friends who have internships are fetching coffee and making copies," she tells me, glancing several times at her laptop as we speak. Clearly she's waiting on something important. "I've been here for about a week, and I think I'm about to land a big account for the company." When I ask her what attracted her to Yes To in the first place, she responds exactly as I expect her to: "Positive energy. The way they've modeled the environment. I'm already more than just a face here."

Yes To is carried internationally in stores that range from posh bou-tiques and department stores in London to high-end luxury stores like

Sephora on the Champs-Elysées in Paris, from mass-market retail chains that include Walgreens, Rite Aid, and Target to health food and specialty stores such as Whole Foods. Their supporters and customers range from celebrities like Rosario Dawson, who attends Seed Fund events on behalf

utes to the opportunity for someone to get an education. As such, something more than *just* another company has been created. This is a shining example of a company that got it *right* by doing it *differently.*

Profit with purpose.

"We're just getting started," Ido excitedly tells me as we say good-bye, which is astonishing to fathom, considering how massive the company has become in such a short period of time. "It takes five years to build a solid business, but we kind of did it backward, starting huge and now laying the groundwork for bigger philanthropic efforts and expansion."

The important point, at least from the cultural and philanthropic angle, isn't that Yes To's financial contribution is so large (many companies donate far more to charitable organizations), but rather that these programs reflect an imbedded corporate philosophy that has been in place since the very beginning. The profit is perpetuating the good as the good perpetuates the profit. A perfect corporate model to aspire to. It is altruistic, symbiotic, *and* profitable. Ido and his team have grown a new breed of company.

*Exactly the type of company that
many of us want to be a part of.*

As I exited the building, I spoke with one last team member—a young accountant named Julie, who had recently graduated from San Diego State University. "I was only applying to companies that were socially responsible," she told me. "I buy conscious, and I try to live that way. I wanted to work for a company that had those same values."

And she is not alone.

↝

HOW WOULD IT feel going to work everyday for a company like MAYA Design? Or Yes To? A company that encourages wearing shorts to work and where you won't be afraid of "speaking out of turn" at the next meeting? These companies are just two of the thousands of companies that are changing capitalism for the better. They are changing the way we conduct business, and they have corporate cultures that are changing the way we work, earn, and even live.

But you still might ask yourself, Why does corporate culture *really* matter that much? Why not just take the job with the highest salary, or the shortest commute, or the most pay for the least amount of work or fewest hours? So what if the work environment is "nurturing?" Maybe you don't care about the orange carpet or the plastic balls or the Nintendo Wii or the silly superheroes or the philanthropic dividends. Maybe you still just want *a* job.

On the day that I was writing this, Tuesday, July 12, 2010, the *New York Times* reported on the front page that BP had a long history of "near misses" and "cutting corners" for the sake of generating the most profit at any cost; a refinery fire in 2005 killed fifteen people in Texas, and a listing oil platform in the Gulf of Mexico had a valve installed backward and poorly welded pipes. They went on to report that in a single inspection of that Texas refinery four years *after* the deadly 2005 fire,

OSHA inspectors *still* found seven hundred safety violations and slapped BP with $87.4 million in fines. It turns out that BP did not have an isolated event in the Gulf of Mexico. They had a corporate culture defined by "profit at any cost."

than Actos for diabetics' hearts, but internal research at SmithKline Beecham suggested that if this information got out it would result in a loss of two hundred million dollars in profit during the two-year period from 2002 to 2004 alone. So, the *New York Times* reported, SmithKline Beecham intentionally suppressed this data for eleven years. They decided it would be better for diabetics to take Avandia and risk damaging their hearts so that the company could generate more profit.

Poor corporate ethos creates negative culture and, in the broadest sense, negative culture hurts everyone.

The reason we should want to work for a company with an orange carpet and a Nintendo Wii, or a room full of plastic balls and silly symbols of recognition, is because these are the markers for a corporate culture and philosophy that leads to happier and healthier employees. The irony is that unhappy employees end up costing businesses a *lot* of money (Gallup reported it to be $416 billion in lost productivity in 2009 alone[24]). So these same elements are also markers for higher corporate profit, and

24. http://money.usnews.com/money/careers/articles/2010/04/14/the-science-of-work place-happiness.

when these companies expand their positive cultural reach to the larger community, they make the world around them better as well.

Which is not to say that a profit-at-any-cost company can't buy some cultural window dressing and attempt to make employees feel good about what they are doing and how they are treated as a route to increased productivity and profits. It does mean, however, that when we are looking for a job, we should be looking for the *right* job at the *right* company, where the culture isn't window dressing but rather genuinely reflects an overriding ethos.

Corporate America, when it chooses to regulate itself, creates a happy workforce and higher profits. That is why corporate culture should matter to all of us, whether we are looking for our next job, thinking about changing careers, or even running our own organizations and companies.

4

...and Focus on the Process

■

Have you got a problem? Do what you can where
you are with what you've got.

THE GAME OF pocket billiards, or pool, is one of the only
"sports" that is played in both bars and highly competitive
professional settings. It is a game that, when played well,
requires executing each individual shot with extreme precision while
simultaneously planning ahead in order to set up each subsequent shot.
The optimum goal in pool is to "run the rack," or run the table—to sink
all of the object balls consecutively.

While the casual pool player might be focused solely on the shot at
hand, or perhaps thinking one or two shots ahead, the great pool players can "see" where every ball on the table is going to be pocketed
almost immediately following the opening break. Talented players will
not only sink the targeted ball(s) with each shot, but they will also have

a game plan in place for the balls remaining on the table. For example, within a few shots of the break, a good player might intentionally cluster all of the balls around one or two of the pockets, which can make winning as easy as shooting fish in a barrel. By simply implementing a strategy, by thinking several potential shots and several *iterations* of potential shots ahead, a player can dramatically increase the odds of winning.

When taking a shot, a good player will put English, or controlled spin, on the cue ball by hitting it in a specific, intentionally off-center location. In so doing, the player not only pockets the initial target ball(s), but also sets up the next shot by sending the cue ball to the optimum spot on the table. In the most ideal situation, a player can consistently place the cue ball so that it is positioned to provide not one, but several viable options for each sequential shot.

> *In the game of pool, the great players*
> *create their own opportunities by*
> *shooting from unique angles.*

The irony is that while putting English on the cue ball in order to pocket a shot might be perceived as more challenging than a straight-on shot that runs the length of the table, it is often *easier* for most players to successfully execute. The reason for this is that when shooting a straight length-of-the-table shot, there is far less control. If the cue strikes even a millimeter too low, or too high, or slightly to the left or right, the target ball can veer off course, negatively altering its trajectory just enough so that it misses the pocket. The cue ball may also stop dead or follow the target ball to a location near a pocket, which most players will tell you is one of the most difficult locations to shoot from. With a straight shot that has veered off course, a player may either miss pocketing the intended target ball altogether and be forced to hand the table over to the opponent or sink the initial target ball but be left in an undesirable position for the next shot. In pool, these seemingly easy "straight shots" can be a deceptively poor choice.

Whether playing 8-ball, the game most commonly played at home or in bars, or 9-ball, the most commonly played tournament game, the goal

ing object balls. Since players also need to consider the potential downside of a poorly executed shot, it is beneficial at times to play a "safety"—a shot in which the shooter is *not* attempting to pocket an object ball at all, but is instead attempting to defensively place the cue ball in an undesirable location for the opponent's upcoming shot.

As players prepare to take each shot, they take a line of sight down the cue stick, and they have to aim with their dominant eye. In order to execute each shot *mechanically*, they must identify, process, and trust the visual information entering their brain from that dominant eye, or they may miscalculate the shot. Novice players will sometimes close their weaker eye in an attempt to block out any confusing visual input from the periphery. Good players take aim with the dominant eye *and* process the information from the periphery successfully. For some people this comes naturally, for others it takes a bit of practice to master.

It quickly becomes clear that in pool it is advantageous to break the game down by analyzing the component parts with a focus on the short-term goal, the long-term goal, the offensive plan, and the defensive strategy—as well as taking into account the mechanics of executing each individual shot. When pool players are able to "see" the entire table at once, when they take aim with their dominant eye and apply English to each of their shots—when they, in effect, deconstruct the game and approach each component step with a strategic plan—they are more likely to win.

One of the commonalities that I observed in my interviews with highly successful individuals, regardless of their backgrounds or areas of expertise, is that many of them implement a very similar strategy in both their professional and personal lives. I noted with striking consistency that success seems to be facilitated when the cognitive approach is analytical and when both problems and opportunities are addressed from a slight angle rather than head-on. This became obvious to me even in cases when the "game strategy" appeared to manifest on a *subconscious* level. For me, this observation reinforced the underlying premise that successful people take relatively ordinary events and respond to them in extraordinary ways. They *think* differently. They "shoot" from an angle and have a natural instinct for trusting their dominant eye. They are able to take a line of sight, process any visual noise from the periphery, act with spot-on accuracy and, in turn, *win*. When utilized in tandem, this is a particular set of skills and cognitive orientation that kindles success.

It seems that individuals who consistently run the table in *life* are able to craft and facilitate career and personal success by employing controlled spin—by putting a little English on each of their metaphorical shots. I also noticed that when this orientation and pattern of thinking are consistently applied to career and life, they can work effectively even if the "player" can't see the entire table at once. And the good news here is that even though many successful people seem to come to these behaviors naturally and on their own, others can learn to do so. By modeling our own behavior in a similar manner, by learning how to approach situations from a slight angle or unique perspective—by striking them just a bit off center—it can open up opportunities for success where we might have thought there were none. In so doing, we can, just like the great pool players, create our own opportunities.

And that may very well be the key to running the table in life.

⤷

.... in him the val-
ues of perseverance and discipline and taught him to be unafraid to think big or to think differently. He was a skateboard kid who loved to analyze the way things work and how to make them simpler and more efficient. "All of those interests I had as a kid resurfaced later, and that's what I work on now," he tells me.

"Kids, when they're young, know what they want. Then people tell them things that derail them. Children should be exposed to their own areas of interest," he says, citing a story based around an experience he had with his elementary school–aged daughter. Finding that she was bored with her summer activities, Bobby asked his daughter what she really loved. The answer? Dogs. "Okay," he reasoned, "if you love dogs, do you want to be a vet? Do you want to go into grooming? Breeding?" Together, they visited several different canine-related enterprises. "We finally watched how they train guide dogs for the blind," says Chang, "and she was like, 'Wow! This is it!' It's like the kids who love building sand castles—let them keep on exploring. Creativity and the sense of play are key to what we, as people, do."

Bobby's early interest in the way things work led him to a career in design and ultimately to a life spent deconstructing challenges as a route to making or designing whatever "it" is *better*. He founded the globally recognized brand Incase in 1997 with a few design friends shortly after completing a stint in marketing at NIKE. Incase developed the first case for what was then a brand-new piece of technology called the iPod for Apple, and from there things took off. More iPod covers, practical laptop cases and bags, and most recently cases for iPhones and iPads. Today Incase is the largest and most recognizable supplier of Apple accessories in the world, and they also engage in a variety of other creative projects, including designing and manufacturing custom guitar cases and bags for musicians who include John Mayer.

At its core, Incase is a company that seeks to utilize high-concept design, creative vision, and engineering to develop simple, more efficient, and aesthetically appealing products. "In the beginning, the whole idea was to play with product to support the new technology that was coming out," Bobby explains to me. "We were literally *playing*. All of a sudden, it turned into a business. We never thought about competition. This allowed us to collaborate with a lot of people. We focused on the fun and creativity over the end result," he emphasizes.

Chang applies the principle of modifying design through what is, essentially, root-cause analysis to bigger concepts than laptop bags and iPad cases. It is, in fact, a broad life philosophy that works for him across disciplines. At the time we spoke, his most recent endeavors included BackNine Studios (a film and media company that develops projects meant to give a voice to "culturally relevant and inspirational storylines"[25]) and H.E.A.L. Together, which creates a platform and network for like-minded charities, nonprofits, and philanthropic organizations to network and integrate, while simultaneously providing complete transparency and sustainability for each organization. He even applies this cognitive approach to activities like golf and bike riding. In fact, Bobby has found success by deconstructing all sorts of challenges to their component parts and then approaching each of them from a unique angle.

Anyone who knows Bobby knows that he is a golf fanatic. He is quite good, from what I have heard. Even if you have not had the pleasure of

---

25. http:// www.back9studios.com.

playing with him, if you talk with him, it is inevitable that you will end up discussing golf. In fact, he is such a respected analytical thinker on the course that golf professionals have consulted him for coaching assistance and guidance when it comes to their swing.

for me. I would either be happy or sad or frustrated. But once I broke it down and focused on and understood the *process*, I was able to lower my score." Chang suggests that by removing the focus from the end result, and by concentrating on and actually enjoying the individual and incremental steps of a particular task—in this case his own golf swing—each of those component parts will be executed with more efficiency. And *that* ultimately leads to greater *overall* success. He goes on to tell me about a time when he was a thirteen handicap (meaning that "par" for him was thirteen more shots than the standard for the course), and after changing his approach to the game, both mechanically and mentally, he was able to shoot one *under* par. That's fourteen shots below his handicap. Anyone who plays golf knows that this is nearly impossible. "I think my friends thought I was cheating or something," he says, and laughs. "But I really just embraced that sort of Zen philosophy of things, enjoyed and focused upon each shot and each *part* of each shot, and *then* the end result was really rewarding." Bobby deconstructed his own golf game, and his score improved by fourteen strokes.

In Miami with Chang a while earlier, he was explaining to me the process of teaching his daughter to ride a bike. He began the task by mentally and physically deconstructing the process of bike riding to its core, which he determined to be balance. After all, most children learn to ride a bike by first using training wheels to keep them balanced. But the problem is, Bobby explained, training wheels don't teach balance. Instead, they provide a temporary crutch that allows children to ride their bikes around even though they can't yet balance on two wheels. "If you look at a problem, isolate the most important element and focus on that. The rest will take care of itself," he says. After all, it takes longer to learn what you are doing right and what you are doing wrong if the feedback you are getting is misleading. With this is mind, he ended up not only removing the training wheels but also lowering the seat—effectively making the bike a "scooter." His student, in this case his own daughter, was then able to learn balance without being misguided by the false sense of accomplishment offered by training wheels, which "catch and correct" before the child begins to fall. By cutting to the core of the task at hand, Bobby was able to drastically reduce the amount of time typically required for the average child to learn to ride a bike. "After we got the balance part down, she was off and riding in no time," he said with a smile.

*Approaching problems, challenges, or opportunities
from unique angles cultivates success.*

༄

BOBBY CHANG SEEMINGLY deconstructs every problem he encounters, or at least those he deems worthy of strategic assessment, to find solutions for real-world situations. The reason that he was able to find success with Incase, as with his other pursuits, whether personal, philanthropic, or even recreational, is that just like the great pool players or golfers, after he deconstructs the "game," he then approaches each aspect analytically and from a unique angle, as opposed to straight on. If one were to take a poll of parents teaching children to ride a bike, very few, if any, would have removed the training wheels. Bobby Chang clearly thinks differently.

Consider, for example, that most companies are highly protective of their designs, but in the early days of Incase, Chang and his partners were not concerned with closely guarding their ideas. In fact, they weren't particularly concerned with the business aspect of the company

results with a faster turnaround rate than their "competitors"—though Bobby would likely be the first to tell you he didn't even think of other companies as competition since, as he put it, they were simply "playing."

Chang approaches every venture and undertaking by knowing what he wants to achieve, but along the way he doesn't *focus* on the end result. Instead, he focuses on the process. This mind-set is something that underpins everything he does. "Any time I have failed, it is because I had focused too intently on the end result instead of *enjoying* the process."

> *When we enjoy the process, and component parts*
> *of each process, we are more likely to find*
> *success, regardless of the situation.*

In all probability, most of us will recognize that our brains don't work exactly like Bobby Chang's. Further, for a lot of us, it takes time to identify what we're "good at," let alone to deconstruct a route to get there. We often aren't able to see the entire table at once, and we might find that we have trouble tuning out the peripheral noise. Yet if we understand that success can be cultivated by learning these skills—by deconstructing our own lives, careers, and opportunities—we can increase our chances of finding success.

⤿

ELLEN GUSTAFSON AND I are sitting in a quiet nook in a downtown San Francisco hotel, talking about everything from elevator music to singing to nutrition in developing nations. Ellen went to college with the intention of becoming "some sort of foreign policy person," as she puts it, majoring in foreign policy and international relations. "I started taking classes about politics in the Middle East, about war and strategy, and I was fascinated by them. For my degree program I had to write a thesis in which I focused on shifting funding from missile defense programs to funding and addressing alternative-threat theories like terrorism."

Ellen already knew some of the theorists and writers who were working in the field of terrorism, and she got an internship with the Council on Foreign Relations during her senior year of college. "That led to a job working for some military officers, so I learned a ton about the military," she says. "Not long after the events of September eleventh I got a serious job at a think tank, but after two years I decided to move out to Los Angeles to become a singer."

Ellen laughs as she recounts taking a cab to a car dealership, purchasing a used car, and moving in with a friend. She didn't exactly have a plan in place. She tells me that shortly after making this decision her parents asked her a very important question. It was a simple question that altered her trajectory in a significant way. "*Why* do you want to be a singer?" they asked. Clearly a legitimate question from caring parents whose daughter had just made quite an abrupt life change. But what Ellen's parents were essentially doing was encouraging her to look at the entire "table." By asking Ellen to identify her endgame, they propelled her to deconstruct the motives behind her actions. After thinking about it and being honest with herself, she came to an interesting conclusion. "My answer wasn't that I really wanted to sing, even though I had studied at Juilliard and loved singing, but that I wanted to become famous so I would have a platform to do humanitarian work and help people," she explains. "It wasn't actually about singing, which was a big realization for me."

Not long after, Ellen headed back East and lent her services to the 2004 Kerry presidential campaign, working at the Democratic National Convention in B

fuel for my life and body, it was profoundly life changing." Excited by this newfound interest, Ellen filled her time reading books, articles, and studies about vitamins, nutrition, cancer, and anything else health related she could get her hands on, becoming more and more interested in the field of nutrition—not as a career or business, but as a way of life. She didn't quite see the entire table yet, but she was beginning to find a line of sight and her dominant eye.

Ellen soon moved back to New York and took a job with ABC News as an investigative reporter specializing in terrorism. Remember, this was her original area of focus while in college. "I was sort of back in my old field, covering terrorism, examining different regions of the world, writing about situations that were happening on planes. When I was there though, I realized that what I was reading in the paper and gravitating toward every morning was *not* about terrorism. It was about nutrition," she explains. "I would look forward to Thursdays, to visit the farmers' market at Lincoln Center and talk to the farmers and eat the fresh food. I was reading every article I could about nutrition, public health, hunger, and obesity." When Ellen pieced this together with all of the other component parts of her life, she realized that her true interest—which had not been evident to her until this moment—was looking at national security and humanitarian issues through the "food lens," as she puts it.

"It suddenly occurred to me that these terrorism hubs that are really angry and unstable are actually really hungry. All of these places I had been learning about for all those years have food security problems— Afghanistan, Pakistan, Myanmar. Then you look at the Horn of Africa, and what we are really talking about is generations upon generations of chronic hunger," Ellen tells me. "Well, eventually that leads to anger, educational problems (you can't learn when you're hungry), and even terrorism. I really began to understand myself in a deep way. I thought, 'I'm really passionate about this and I *have* to work in this space.'"

With this newfound realization about herself, Ellen looked at organizations that did domestic food work, and soon found a job opening at the United Nations World Food Programme. "I had none of the qualifications—they wanted someone with a master's degree and years of experience," Ellen tells me. But she sold them on her talents and knowledge. She told her future employers that even though she lacked the traditional education and experience they were looking for, she made up for it through self-education, enthusiasm, and her unique approach. "And I got the job," she says.

> *Approaching a typically traditional space from*
> *a unique angle can create opportunity where*
> *opportunity did not previously exist.*

"I *thought* I wanted to work in national security—the CIA, the State Department, or the NSA—but at the end of the day, I realized that this wasn't the stuff I was reading about," Ellen tells me. To this end, she suggests doing an experiment for two weeks. "Open the paper or go online and find an article that you're interested in. Whatever catches your eye. Maybe it's Obama's Iran policy. But you might find that you only make it halfway through the article before you jump over to the arts section or the business section and read entire articles. Or vice versa. This is a great way to understand who you really are," she explains, "and to get away from what you *think* you're supposed to be, or supposed to like, or supposed to do. This process can relieve a lot of stress and lead to working

tering areas of personal interest by implementing a unique approach outweighed the graduate degrees that she was competing against for the job. "Read a lot. And because you want to. Not because you're forcing yourself to cram," she advises. "I can talk to anyone about food policy because I have educated myself about it and it's what I truly love. I don't need to prepare—it's in my blood now. It's who I am."

Ellen is, in effect, giving the same advice as Bobby Chang. She is telling us to identify what we want to do, even if it takes a while to figure out what that is, and to then approach it from a new angle—with a bit of our own spin.

When Ellen began working at the UN, the initiative she became most attracted to was the school feeding program. "Quite frankly, when you look at food aid as it is traditionally employed, it's not that appealing," she explains. "You're essentially dumping subpar food on people who may or may not be receiving it. School feeding is entirely different. I believe it's the most brilliant way of moving people past poverty. By providing kids with meals that are nutrient fortified, they are able to focus on schoolwork—and they are also drawn to *actually attend school* because of the free meal."

Ellen, who was working at the UN as a public information officer, joined forces with Lauren Bush, who was an honorary spokesperson for the United Nations World Food Programme at the time, and together they decided to take on the issue of school feeding in a big way and on their own. "Lauren designed this tote bag, and it was amazing," she tells me. "We thought that if we could manufacture and sell a line of bags that could generate significant funds for school feeding, we could make an impact on the problem."

Ellen and Lauren first brought the concept to their employer. "The UN passed on our project initially, and basically everyone else we went to said no when it came to support and financing. We had every wall up against us in every single way—we were facing this massive bureaucracy."

But rather than give up, Ellen and Lauren approached the issue from a different angle and changed the course of not only their lives but also of the lives of millions of children across the world. "I literally turned to her (Lauren) one day and said, 'I think we should start our own company. Let's just do it ourselves.' I'm pretty sure she thought I was completely nuts, but we did it." And so in 2007 their company, FEED Projects, was launched out of Ellen's apartment. "It's crazy," Ellen says, "how much has happened in such a short amount of time."

The pair wanted to get the initial line of bags out in time for the holidays, so they rented a minivan, removed the backseats, loaded it with their first shipment of bags (that had just arrived via plane), drove it through customs at John F. Kennedy Airport in New York, and brokered the customs bill with one of Ellen's personal checks for four hundred dollars. That same customs officer purchased a bag on the spot because he was so impressed with what they were doing. "He was our first customer!" Ellen recalls, laughing.

"Everyone told us that we couldn't do all of these things. And we just did them anyway. We had visited schools in Rwanda and become so inspired. The Rwandan people who are facilitating school feeding for those kids are complete heroes for what they are doing, and no one knew about it," she says. "Our goal was to create a fashion item that helps raise awareness for what these people are doing—that's what this was, and still is, all about."

Ellen and Lauren started FEED Projects to address the global issue of child hunger and malnutrition. Today FEED designs and sells bags

.... gets to choose not only the bag but the world hunger issue that each bag is paired with as well. These are big, high-concept, child-saving, life-altering totes and bags.

One interesting and compelling aspect about the story of FEED is the major development in 2010, when they entered into a partnership with the Gap to carry their products. But what interested me even more as I was sitting with Ellen that afternoon in San Francisco was that in the three years *prior* to this collaboration with the Gap, FEED had already sold well over half a million bags, provided meals for *fifty-five million* children across the world, and generated millions of dollars in revenue. And perhaps of equal interest, up until this point, the entire business had basically been run out of an apartment with only four employees. On top of that, FEED had a relatively negligible social media presence and managed to avoid spending any money on traditional advertising. One has to wonder how on earth something this huge and world changing had come out of something seemingly so small, and how it happened so fast.

"We are in our third year, and we *just* hired our fifth person," Ellen tells me twenty-four hours before the Gap launch party. "We have done something like eighteen million dollars in sales and given away six million dollars. We give so much money away that we are giving away our profits. I can't even believe it. We're going on HSN[26] soon," she enthuses.

26. Home Shopping Network.

(In fact, Lauren Bush would be on HSN a few weeks later, selling a special run of Halloween-themed FEED bags.) "We did it backward. We were in Whole Foods, for example, but had no online presence. It's been a funny dance—we've never paid for advertising, we have never paid a celebrity to wear our bags, we've never sent a free bag to a celebrity. (Reese Witherspoon, among many others, has been seen sporting the bags.) All of our publicity is just old-school, heartfelt, good old American press. If people like us, and want to do an article or push what we are doing, then we do it. And it gets us into the next magazine or retailer—*Vogue* or whoever else."

Much like Bobby Chang and his partners at Incase in the early days, Ellen says, "We had no business model. No idea what we were doing businesswise." In fact, according to Ellen, FEED was losing seven cents a bag when they first started. "We were more focused on the kids we wanted to help than we were with running an efficient business at the beginning. We've now backed into running an efficient business, which was a really cool way to do it, I think." Just like Incase, FEED developed as a concept to create a solution to a root problem or need, and the business aspects fell into place as they grew.

The press and the public became passionate about FEED because of the simplicity of the message, the profound nature of the cause, and the enormous appeal of what it offered—a direct solution to a daunting problem. Whether the cost of the bag is perceived to be a charitable donation and the bag itself a token gift for that donation, or if the bag is purchased for its design and the donation to charity is an added benefit, the concept of making a specific, direct, and quantifiable contribution— school lunches for children in this case—is enormously appealing to many consumers. As long as it is in use, the bag itself also functions as an advertisement for the company and the movement, just as the ongoing use of the bag provides a perpetual feel-good dividend to the consumer. Regardless of how you choose to deconstruct the business model, and by any of the metrics used to measure success, marketing a consumer-driven product to create a sustainable way to combat global issues like hunger and malnutrition is a triumphant accomplishment.

"Our business model was using big retailers to get our products out there," Ellen tells me. "A lot of people develop a website and then push that website, selling a few products at a time. We have sold almost six hundred thousand bags but have only six thousand followers on Face-book, for ...

... carried in twelve countries. Now we have a fashion brand, and a few years ago I was this nerdy policy wonk. It's amazing."

All the while, Ellen's passion for food and nutrition has only grown. "It's not just about ending hunger, but about nutrition and sustainable agriculture and all these other tangential issues."[27] The team looked at FEED and asked themselves how they could expand the program to affect issues closer to home and outside the arena of international hunger. "Lauren and I had been talking about getting involved with domestic school food for years. We thought, if we're going to go that route, it can't just be about hunger. It has to be about the nutritional value of the food that we are giving our kids. So the new program at the Gap is all about getting healthier school food to kids across America. We are so committed to this, and people respond to that passion. It's not work. It's what we love. I live, eat, and breathe this stuff. It makes me so happy."

27. In 2012 Ellen founded Change Dinner (Formerly the 30 Project), "a new way to connect global hunger and obesity and crowd-source long-term food system change." She also cofounded FoodTank with Danielle Nierenberg, an initiative that aims to "bridge the domestic and global food issues by highlighting how hunger, obesity, climate change, unemployment, and other problems can be solved by more research and investment in agriculture."

ELLEN LOOKED AT the issue of terrorism from a unique angle and took the "training wheels" off. And one of the root causes she identified when she deconstructed terrorism was hunger. From its inception in 2007, to a mere three years later when I sat down with Ellen in August of 2010, FEED was taken from a concept with a single product design to a successful company that is playing a significant role in the international battle against childhood hunger and malnutrition. Ellen and Lauren accomplished this feat by deconstructing the problem *and* the route to the solution, then attacking both from an unconventional angle. In so doing, they circumvented the traditional pathways and barricades that have typically plagued the food distribution space and managed to create their own opportunities as they put healthy, nutrient-rich food directly into the hands and stomachs of millions of children around the world, while simultaneously doing what they love.

What Ellen found when she deconstructed her own life is arguably equally as interesting. As Ellen was telling me the story of FEED, she was also telling me her own story: an indisputable journey of growth, self-discovery, and ultimately, extraordinary success. As we spoke, I thought back to Bobby Chang's observation that many people, like him, know what they love to do from a young age. Even though Ellen took a more serpentine route to get to where she was going, even though her true interest wasn't evident to her as a child, she was in the process of discovering that interest the entire time. And both Ellen and Bobby approached their chosen fields with more than a little bit of "English."

As Ellen demonstrates in her own story, and as Bobby demonstrates in his analysis of challenges, if we deconstruct a problem or an opportunity to its component parts and then approach it from a new and unique angle, an equally new and unique solution is waiting to be unearthed. And both of their stories illustrate that there are many ways in which to approach any specific field of interest, especially when we recognize that we don't necessarily have to approach the target straight on.

This very methodical and analytical approach to problem solving proves to be virtually universally applicable—not only when building

WHEN THIRTY-THREE MINERS who had been trapped for sixty-nine days in a collapsed copper mine two thousand feet beneath the ground in the northern Atacama Desert near Copiapó, Chile, were safely rescued in October of 2010, it was, by every measure, a rescue effort of unprecedented success. Never before had there been an evacuation of miners trapped from this deep beneath the earth's surface, nor had men ever survived for this length of time—over two months— entombed in the ground. The rescue mission, which was spearheaded by the Chilean government, involved the collaborative participation of many different nations, numerous corporations and organizations, and hundreds of individuals.

Help came in various forms, ranging from the critical emotional support provided by the family members who camped out next to the mine to be close to their loved ones to the high-tech expertise of a wide variety of specialists from around the world. The rescue tunnel was bored through thousands of feet of rock by a high-speed drill provided by Schramm, Inc., a West Chester, Pennsylvania, company whose CEO saw the story of the trapped men and the mine collapse on the news and called to offer help. A second company, this one from Berlin, Pennsylvania, called Center Rock, Inc., provided the drill bits.

NASA offered design advice for the escape capsule that was being constructed to transport the men through one of the three narrow shafts simultaneously being drilled through the rock, and offered further expertise culled from decades of work with astronauts routinely confined in small spaces. They sent design ideas, reportedly seventy-five different possibilities for the escape capsule alone, as well as advice pertaining to the medical and psychological issues that might plague the trapped miners. Experts in drilling technology were flown in from Argentina and the United States; a special cable for the escape hatch came from Germany; and assistance arrived in all shapes and forms from countries around the globe as far away as South Africa and Spain.

The rescue team had contingency plan after contingency plan in place. They also had to address each individual step in the rescue process, from how to monitor the health of the trapped miners to how to ensure their safe transit through the escape tunnel, and from how to assist and support the miners' families to how to handle the media should the efforts not go well. By all accounts the Chilean government handled this catastrophic situation with both unwavering fortitude and enormous decorum, despite the poor prospects they faced for success. The emotionally charged and highly technical task of saving these men involved the coordination of countless independent organizations and resources—as well as the aforementioned management of the families and the media—from the first news of the mine collapse to the successful extraction of all of the miners.

Throughout the event there was no governmental finger-pointing and no internal bickering—at least none that found its way into the mainstream press. There was only one single-minded focus—to bring the trapped miners to safety—and every single stage of this rescue mission was methodically planned and perfectly executed. After sixty-nine days, all thirty-three men, plus the six rescue workers that descended into the mine to assist them, emerged to safety in a seamless, hiccup-free, near flawless venture. The successful resolution of this disaster led many to openly question how the Chilean government succeeded in the management of this rescue, when many other countries with more significant resources at their disposal have handled similar catastrophic situations often with significantly poorer outcomes. The answer is simple: the government stepped in and took immediate control of the situation, claimed ownership ~f +h

...p~~ ... Chile. In fact,

... taking even a cursory glance at the steps implemented by the Chilean government to save the trapped miners, it looks a lot like the route to success detailed by Bobby Chang. While never losing sight of the end goal—saving the miners—the focus remained not only on the process as a whole but also on each *step* therein. The problem was deconstructed into its component parts, and every iteration thereof was approached one by one with unwavering focus.

During the rescue mission, the Chilean government's primary concern for the end goal, saving the men, was never derailed by peripheral noise. They didn't look to blame the mining company for safety violations (of which there were many), and there was never any open debate over the enormous cost associated with the rescue. Accomplishing a task of this magnitude mandated that virtually every decision be approached from a unique and calculated angle. Technology had to be modified and adapted in order to achieve success, and experts of different backgrounds had to collaborate on a time-sensitive and creative level—all with human lives on the line. Remember, a rescue mission of this scope and magnitude was something that had never even been attempted before, let alone successfully executed.

If the true route to success lies in the perfect execution of each of the component parts of any given task along the way, then those handling the rescue of the thirty-three trapped miners in Chile ran the table. Contrast this with the rescue efforts after Hurricane Katrina, in which every government agency in the United States failed again and again— from the local New Orleans police to the White House to FEMA— because they were collectively overwhelmed by the larger problem and lost sight of the end goal. These groups became more focused on bureaucratic finger-pointing and self-preservation than on actually helping anyone, and as a result they got lost in the peripheral noise.

The route to success outlined here is applicable not only to pool and golf, or to individuals building careers or starting multi-million-dollar companies like Incase or FEED Projects, but also to governments handling disasters—or almost any other situation. The approach to both challenges and opportunities that seems to come so naturally to successful individuals also seemed to come naturally to the government and the rescue workers in Chile. For the rest of us, it should become one component of the model blueprint for achieving success.

With a single-minded focus on each step in the process, we can discover new angles from which to approach and solve problems.

We can, in turn, create our own opportunities for success.

5

Define Your Fire

■

A man's growth is seen in the successive choirs of
his friends.

—RALPH WALDO EMERSON

I N 2006, AT the open invitation of CEO Reed Hastings, tens of
thousands of engineers, statisticians, mathematicians, and computer scientists from around the world began collaborating in
small groups on what would become an almost three-year-long competition to improve the algorithm that Netflix had been using to recommend films to its existing customers. Many of the team members had
never met each other, and in some cases they even lived on different
continents—but they enthusiastically formed alliances and volunteered
their time as they joined forces to compete against other groups in a
skunkworks-style project for a potential prize of one million dollars.

At the time, the algorithm used by Netflix to recommend films to
viewers was heavily based on the previous rental patterns and the

subsequent viewing preferences of customers who had selected the same movies in the past. Hastings designed the contest so that the first individual or team to improve the success rate of this algorithm by 10 percent would receive the million-dollar prize. While numerous groups worked for years on the project, a seven-member team called BellKor's Pragmatic Chaos was the first to submit a winning formula, beating the contenders who came in second place by less than half an hour. Although both of these teams had succeeded in finding a way to improve the Netflix algorithm by the required 10 percent, BellKor's Pragmatic Chaos reached the finish line just a few minutes ahead of the competition. Everyone else, in excess of twenty thousand teams of mathematicians and computer scientists, had been working for Netflix for free.

If Netflix had hired twenty thousand teams to accomplish the task, and assuming each team had, on average, four members earning a salary of seventy-five thousand dollars each, it would have cost the company roughly six *billion* dollars in salaries alone, assuming that each member worked full-time for one year on the project instead of part-time for three years. Through this challenge, Hastings was able to assemble an extraordinarily large group of experts by utilizing the availability of connective technology, while simultaneously capitalizing on human nature and our insatiable desire to compete. He then leveraged this highly motivated talent pool in an effort to build Netflix's corporate profit for what was, unquestionably, a bargain basement price.

Executives at several companies, including AT&T, allowed a few of their employees to participate in the Netflix contest while on their own corporate payrolls, believing that these employees would receive significant educational value from the experience that the companies could then leverage and monetize themselves. But for the most part, the team members were volunteering their free time. All of the individuals working to refine the Netflix algorithm knew the odds were stacked against them when they signed on for the project and that they were, in all probability, not going to win the million dollars. They knew that, for all intents and purposes, they were working for a profitable corporation entirely for free.

There have been many ~~~~~~ ~~~~~~~~~~~~~~~~~~~~~~ ~~~~~~~~~~ that would serve the greater good. By outsourcing the research and development (R&D) as an open competition, Hastings challenged the existing employment model and corporate pay scale, getting the results he needed in an ingenious manner. Further, he accomplished it at a fraction of the cost and in a fraction of the time it would normally have taken a company like Netflix to develop a successful modification to their algorithmic-based, content-recommendation model. To boot, Hastings set up the challenge in such a way that he wouldn't have to pay a penny to any of the tens of thousands of highly educated and skilled team members who were working on the project if none of the groups succeeded in meeting the required 10 percent improvement to the company's current algorithm. A million-dollar prize is clearly irresistible to most individuals yet, in many cases, is pocket change in the world of corporate R&D.

At the other end of the spectrum, Amazon has a work-for-hire site called Mechanical Turk that pairs incredibly small outsourced jobs that they call "HITs"[28] with anyone who agrees to complete the tasks, many of which may only take a few minutes to accomplish. Review a product, transcribe an audio recording, caption a picture, or rewrite a sentence— just to cite a handful of examples—and one can earn anywhere from a

---

28. Human intelligence tasks.

few pennies to a few dollars, depending on the complexity of the task and how well it's been executed. Interested parties can sign up, do as much or as little as they choose, make their own hours, and work from home—or from their office during "free time," as they double dip and simultaneously collect a paycheck from their primary employer. Turk users give the site mixed reviews; some seem to be able to eke out a few hundred dollars a week by working from their own computers and completing an endless series of minuscule component tasks, whereas others view it as deceptive and exploitative—providing what amounts to below-minimum-wage pay.

What the Netflix competition did, and what the ongoing Amazon work-for-hire site is currently doing, is engaging in—and monetizing—unique forms of crowdsourcing.

⌐

CROWDSOURCING IS A term that was originally identified by Jeff Howe in a 2006 *Wired* article. He would go on to define the term as "the act of a company or institution taking a function once performed by employees and outsourcing it to an undefined (and generally large) network of people in the form of an open call."[29] While the term itself is relatively new, a neologism born out of technology-facilitated interconnectivity, the concept of problem solving through intellectual outsourcing has been in practice for quite some time. In the early eighteenth century the British government offered the Longitude Prize to anyone who could assist the navy in finding a better way to navigate and trace the movement of its ships. In the nineteenth century the *Oxford English Dictionary* was compiled through millions of submissions from individuals of diverse backgrounds from all over the world, just to cite a couple of examples.

29. http://crowdsourcing.typepad.com/cs/2006/06/crowdsourcing_a.html.

Exploiting crowds is, in fact, currently creating pools of cheap labor for giant corporations in a multitude of ways. For example, uTest, with clients like Microsoft and Google, is applying the crowdsourcing model to find bugs in new software. And just as Netflix did in their contest, uTest is achieving results f[...]

[...] productive are paid. Thus, this competitive, pay-only-for-results model is drastically reducing the cost of doing business while accelerating the time frame for obtaining actionable results.

Perhaps one of the earliest and most well-known stories of online-based crowdsourcing is the global initiative to coordinate the donation of idle computer power by inviting individuals to download a program to their personal computers that allowed SETI@home[31] to use their central processing units (CPUs) when the individual computer owners were not using the devices themselves. SETI then used the donated and aggregate CPUs to search for extraterrestrial life-forms by monitoring deep space for radio waves.

There are now numerous entities that solicit idle CPUs much in the same way that Turk is soliciting idle workforce time. By breaking down large scientific tasks into fragmented pieces that can be farmed out to individual computers that are not in use, these initiatives can harness that collective power to create a piecemeal "supercomputer" that is capable of completing massive tasks one CPU at a time. A company called D2OL uses donated personal computer power to find agents to

---

30. http://www.computerweekly.com/Articles/2009/07/30/237121/Crowdsourcing-slashes-software-testing-time.html.

31. http://www.pcworld.com/article/5198/you_can_help_search_for_signs_of_intel ligent_life.html.

counter biological terrorism; Harvard University's Clean Energy Project is searching for molecules to reduce our dependence on fossil fuels; and FightAIDS@Home is using the donated computer time to research drug-resistant HIV. Anyone can go to the World Community Grid[32] (which works as an umbrella group for many of these projects), sign up to donate idle computer time, and thus become part of the supercomputer CPU "crowd"—serving the collective good with the promise of the potential for maximum output for what amounts to a minuscule amount of personal effort.

As connective technology is reducing the number of jobs in certain industries and changing the pay structures for others in creative ways, it is also simultaneously creating new opportunities in other fields. The net gain in jobs after any new technology settles in is likely to be greater than what previously existed, but during the transition job opportunities are lost in some areas while they open up in others. As corporate giants are spending millions of dollars to ascertain how to utilize the crowd as a resource to increase revenue and expedite results, the question becomes how the rest of us can use these same unprecedented opportunities offered by connectivity to source our own crowds for personal advancement.

In order to source the crowd for personal gain we must first align ourselves with the "right crowd," and then harness the scope and depth of its potential power.

Building a personal network is nothing new. Joining a professional society or a club, volunteering with a local community group, maintaining ties to faith-based institutions, alumni associations, elite schools and clubs, or attending conferences in order to build connections for future opportunities are all forms of old-fashioned networking. While none of

32. http://www.worldcommunitygrid.org.

this is new *conceptually*, connective technology has made crowdsourcing significantly broader in terms of reach and infinitely easier to execute from a *practical* standpoint. Most notably though, it is clear that the real power of technology-based crowdsourcing differentiates it in a substantive way from old-fashioned

Just as connectivity-based crowdsourcing has been successfully harnessed by computer scientists for the collective good and utilized by corporations in financially creative manners to increase profit, crowdsourcing can also be used in equally profound ways by *individuals*. Further, unlike old-fashioned networking, which is often restrictive, exclusionary, and encumbered with socioeconomic and geographic "gates," the new model of connectivity-based crowdsourcing can be strikingly egalitarian and meritocratic. Yet the fact is that many of us are using this potentially powerful set of tools either ineffectively or for relatively trivial pursuits. We use Facebook to catalogue our social lives and sign up for career-based sites that often function as registers for counting connections and nothing more, but miss the opportunity to develop and maintain relationships that can generate career leverage or exothermic power.

> *In so doing, we may be missing the opportunity to build the personal networks that are necessary for crafting the careers, the lifestyles, and ultimately the success that we are seeking.*

⌒

IN 2005 JESSICA JACKLEY cofounded Kiva Microfunds, which in a few short years has grown to become one of the world's most recognizable microlending organizations. Successfully challenging the structural, social, and economic factors that underpin institutionalized poverty in many developing countries, Kiva utilizes, in a groundbreaking manner, connective technology to crowdsource—or more specifically, crowdfund—the financial needs of marginalized individuals, many of whom live on less than a few dollars a week.

Microcredit, or a microloan, is simply a small loan designed to provide either for a basic service or to facilitate entrepreneurship as a means to lift the recipient(s) out of poverty. This concept was first developed by Muhammad Yunus, who won the Nobel Peace Prize along with the Grameen Bank in 2006, "for their efforts to create economic and social development from below."[33] Yunus was lifting people from poverty through the use of microloans in Bangladesh, and he created the Grameen Bank to facilitate these loans. In the case of Kiva, ordinary people (as opposed to banks) become potential interest-free lenders by joining the Kiva community and browsing the profiles of potential loan recipients,[34] who might include a woman in Uganda who needs five hundred dollars for her basket-making business, a man in Brazil who needs a small loan to expand his taxi service, or a family in Kenya that needs money to purchase a cow. Lenders can loan the entire amount requested or agree to commit as little as twenty-five dollars toward the overall fund-raising goal. Kiva reports roughly a 98.9 percent payback rate on all loans, and if the lender chooses to do so, after the initial loan is repaid, the same microdollars can be loaned over and over again, effectively creating a library of funds that function as a

---

33. http://www.nobelprize.org.
34. Sometimes these are people who have already received loans thru a microfinance institution (MFI). Since the Kiva lending community has grown to be so large, MFIs frequently make the loans *in advance,* and Kiva repays them after the member loans are made.

renewable, recyclable commodity—a perpetual source of private working capital to progressively leverage individuals and families from extreme poverty—rendering the system inherently sustainable.

Kiva established a new model that single-handedly harnesses the exo-

hundred dollars. They have effectively democratized the crowd, removing many of the seemingly impenetrable barriers that have served to entrench poverty in communities around the world and function to restrict access to capital on geographic-, socioeconomic-, and gender-based biases.[35]

The concept for Kiva began to develop in the spring of 2004, and by April of 2005 the organization funded their first seven microloans (a total of thirty-five hundred dollars), all of which were repaid in full by the following September. That October, with the initial loans repaid, Kiva officially launched as a nonprofit. By December of 2006, two million dollars in microloans had changed hands and Kiva was lauded in the *Year in Ideas* section of the *New York Times Magazine*. Less than a year later, in August of 2007, the organization surpassed ten million dollars in loans, and that September Kiva was featured in President Bill Clinton's book *Giving,* with Jessica Jackley and Kiva cofounder Matt Flannery appearing on *The Oprah Winfrey Show* with the former president. Within six months of *that*, a total of twenty-five million dollars had been loaned through Kiva's community. Eight months later, the fifty-million-dollar mark was surpassed as Kiva's exponential growth

35. Over 80 percent of the entrepreneurs who have received microloans though Kiva are women.

continued to demonstrate, rather dramatically, the connective, exothermic power of an engaged community.

Kiva managed to break down geographic, cultural, sociopolitical, and corporate barriers by crowdsourcing their way toward changing the fundamentals of lending, forging unprecedented relationships between lenders and loan recipients, and affecting hundreds of thousands living in poverty. Within a few years of its launching, Kiva has generated well over a hundred million dollars in microloans for the world's poor and is rapidly approaching the two-hundred-million-dollar mark. By successfully executing a solution to a global problem proven to be unsolvable by conventional means, the model used by Kiva demonstrates the potentially stunning power of crowdsourcing.

At its core, what Kiva does is technology-based crowdfunding with a brilliantly crafted *personal* connection. As potential loan recipients present information about themselves—which includes pictures, how much money they are asking for (the average "ask" is $381),[36] an explanation of why they need the funding, and what they are going to do with it once received—their profiles become visible to the Kiva lending community. The visual aspect of being able to actually *see* the people who are requesting loans, and the resultant sense of community that Kiva creates, enables microfinanciers to become emotionally vested in the people to whom they are lending.

When building our own networks, the quality of
our relationships is what matters most.

As technologically driven as Kiva's form of crowdsourcing is, it is also designed to forge a strong personal connection between the lender and the recipient of the funds. And this is something that Jessica Jackley made very clear to me when we began to discuss her work.

36. http://www.kiva.org.

"There is an aspect of certain transactions between a donor and a recipient that can cause very unhealthy power dynamics in terms of the way people start to see each other as better or worse, strong or weak," Jessica tells me as we sit down at a corner table for lunch at a tofu res-

cial and lead to more substantive long-term positive results than a "handout" or donation. The money might be the same, but the relationship forged through a loan differs quite dramatically from one established with a charitable gift.

Jessica goes on to explain how this power dynamic works in both directions. Not only can the recipient of a donation become psychologically diminished by the charitable transaction but in many ways the donor can as well. Even though Kiva was not the first to isolate this flaw in the structure we have built around addressing need, it was able to provide an actionable model that circumvented it by empowering both parties instead. And they were able to introduce this model to the marketplace with remarkable success.

"When I give you a loan, as opposed to a donation, it's an expression of confidence," Jessica tells me. "It's a message. It's saying, 'I believe in you. You can pay me back.' When I give you a loan, I'm promoting a partnership of equality, a relationship of dignity and respect, and you are my business partner—not the recipient of my donation. Don't get me wrong," she says, "there are lots of amazing donations with dignity. But loans *can* be far more empowering. There's this participation in someone else's story, this participation in the next chapter.

"If I give you something, even if it's a donation of dignity, you might tell me how things are going for a while, but the exchange is *done*. With a loan, the exchange continues over time, as I not only transfer the funds to you, but then as you slowly pay me back. I become even more emotionally vested in your story and progress," Jessica explains, quick to point out the value of a "real exchange," as she puts it. "It gives me this different excuse to pay more attention to you." This is exactly where most of us fail with the use of social networking tools, through which we engage emotionally with friends and family, but fail to do so with our potential business relationships.

"When I was planning for my TED[37] talk, I decided that I wasn't going to stand up there and try to convince everyone that it's so meaningful to give—I think we all know that. I don't think people need to be convinced," Jessica tells me. "The problem is that we want to be useful and meaningful in each other's lives, but we become afraid. We are either told that these problems aren't going away, or that our little effort isn't enough. When we're thanked for our small contribution to a nonprofit, the next 'ask' is often 'there's more to do,' or 'you should give more'—we are almost never given the feeling that we've done enough. And why should we? We start to feel inadequate when we see commercial after commercial reminding us that 'for the cost of a cup of coffee, you could be saving a child's life'—that's a very defeating thing to hear, and somewhat insulting to a person who has just been motivated by the overwhelming problem in the world that's just been described," she says. "So, the problem is huge, but all we need from you is a quarter or a dollar thirty-nine, and everything will be fine? Really?"

After we briefly derail our discussion to hypothesize how the chef gets the tofu chicken wings onto the mini-skewers, Jessica dives passionately back into the conversation. "Don't give me an option that is so small when you've asked me to rise to the occasion," she says, "and now all you are asking me for is pocket change? And I won't even notice it? I

---

37. Technology, Entertainment, Design.

want to notice it. I want to feel it. I want to be meaningful. Give me the privilege and the dignified honor and option of actually giving something meaningful and real. Something tangible. When they say 'the cost of a cup of coffee,'" she explains, "what they are really saying is

.... distinction.

Time, knowledge, and participation in each other's stories are all viable forms of currency, which is a critical element to remember when crowdsourcing and networking in our own lives.

Jessica is now applying many of these same crowdsourcing, crowdfunding, and community engagement principles to her most recent venture, ProFounder. ProFounder serves as a platform for entrepreneurs and small businesses based in the United States to generate capital through a peer network sourced privately through the entrepreneur's own group of friends and family, or publicly through the general ProFounder community, who see the business plan presented through the ProFounder website. Unlike Kiva, these transactions aren't loans. They are actual investments in specific businesses with a potential return of revenue based on the financial success of the businesses over a set number of years—sometimes with the added bonus of a deal on products or services that the businesses provide.

ProFounder is an evolution and derivative of Jessica's previous project as she moves toward sourcing a different crowd—this time with an eye toward modifying the institutionalized structure of banking, venture capitalism, start-up funding, and small business investing for a *profitable* return. But ProFounder, just like Kiva, is focused on engaging supportive communities around entrepreneurs in order to provide the various resources that they need for growth. Again, capital is not solely defined as financial currency. ProFounder provides a platform that perpetuates relationships among these individuals and allows contributors—investors, lenders, and advisers—to participate in the story of a company, as well as, potentially, the profits. Jessica and I go on to discuss both leveling the playing field in terms of an individual's power to invest in small businesses, and also the ability of businesses to affect institutionalized norms.

"Laws and regulations exist that limit people's ability to invest in the United States in unnecessary ways, so not everyone gets to play. If you want to invest in a small business, how do you do that?" Jessica asks in response to the question of what niche ProFounder fills. "Unless it's a publicly traded company, it's not easily done. How do you invest in a friend's start-up company while he is simultaneously raising money from a venture capital firm? You'll get shut out. The people with the most money often dictate the terms and don't want smaller investors," she explains. "We want to open this up so that everyone can have a chance to empower a great business, and so that every entrepreneur can have the opportunity to get the resources they need without selling their soul to some big firm that doesn't really know them or care about them over the long haul. The wrong people are being empowered.

"The best way to create great relationships, or even to galvanize relationships that already exist with friends, family, or community members, is to allow investors to *actually* invest and participate in the upside," Jessica enthuses. "That's exciting because if the business does well, you'll do well. So *that*, I think, is the fitting relationship. All of these things are the same expression of what I believe in terms of engaging a community to come around an entrepreneur and empower them and support them."

*In this same sense, we can engage the networks in our own
lives and in our own stories without asking for a single
penny. We must simply cultivate a crowd that recycles,
in a reciprocal and productive manner, the exchange*

.... goal, she says. They want the love *and* the money. It's money and intention. It's money and encouragement. It's money and meaning."

~

IN THE CASE of Kiva, the crowd is generating interest-free loans for the world's poor. Jessica was able to help curate entrepreneurial success while retooling the psychological dynamics that revolve around the lender and the recipient of need-based capital. When these ideas are applied in the for-profit space, in this case with ProFounder, she is able to adjust the crowdsourcing model and transition from international loans to domestic investments. By helping small businesses grow, by providing resources and enabling previously uninvited investors to participate in the potential growth and profit of entrepreneurs, she is opening the door to what has been a closed system. Essentially, both Kiva and ProFounder serve to source two different crowds and two different sets of dynamics to create exothermic results.

When I ask her about the switch from the nonprofit to the for-profit side of the fence, Jessica tells me she sees it as a natural evolution. "It's a different application, but with the same principles and the same concepts. It's a different market with a different tool," she explains. "So that's interesting and I am learning. Social change can happen in almost any organizational structure. Being a 501(c)3 is a tax code, not a religion. There are for-profit businesses that are doing a ton of good in the world, and there are nonprofits, for example, that are screwing things up," Jessica tells me. "We don't need to be bound by that organizational structure."

The common denominator in Jessica's success seems to be how she sees and builds connections between people. And this is evident in her personal network as well. That afternoon, Jessica insisted that I work out of her home office for the rest of the day and attend a party she was hosting that evening. It was a tough invitation to resist, especially considering that my plan was to work back at my hotel. "It's going to be epic," she told me enthusiastically. "There are a bunch of people that I want you to meet."

That night, as I met some of the people in her network, I couldn't help but notice how diverse the group was. Despite the relatively small nature of the get-together, maybe twenty-five people or so, there wasn't a uniform demographic at all. Guests ranged from world-renowned scholar and cohost Reza Aslan and actress Heather Graham to film industry executives, poets, computer programmers, entrepreneurs, and humanitarians. And while they were all having fun, they were also networking, talking about big ideas, exchanging information, and referring each other to *their* friends and networks.

> *Considering how fundamentally life altering, on an individual and collective basis, some forms of crowdsourcing can be, and how significant the role and the power of the "right" crowd is, all of us should reassess how we craft the networks in our own lives.*

〜

AS I LEFT Jessica's party, ducking out a bit early to catch the red-eye to Boston, I began thinking about historical time periods that have resulted in significant physical or intellectual migration and the fact that we are in the midst of one now. During the Industrial Revolution of the eighteenth and nineteenth centuries, which began in England and spread around the globe, the city of Manchester emerged as one of the world's

…… ..υ... υυαι ω eiectricity—led to demand for improved transit, which mandated the construction of better roadways, railways, and canals.

Although the catalyst for this striking global change was a handful of technological advances in conjunction with a new economic philosophy and banking system, the consequences of which were almost immeasurable, what was quantifiable at the time was substantially enhanced productivity, a massive increase in income for the middle classes, and the fact that the Industrial Revolution manifested as tangible *physical* change. It involved the building of factories, the invention and construction of machines, the relocation of people, and the transport of goods and materials. This generated smog and noise and massive transitional movement, making the Industrial Revolution impossible to miss.

By contrast, the technological revolution of the 1980s was far less noticeable in the physical sense, and although it incrementally crept into the homes and offices of virtually every sector of life and business, its impact on the job front at the time centered on a sector of the population predominantly involved in computer technology. While the technology boom of the 1980s didn't *change* most jobs per se, it certainly facilitated them. Decades later, the connectivity revolution has reached a level parallel to that of the Industrial Revolution in at least one particularly compelling way. While the connectivity revolution is *physically* stationary—it doesn't involve laying railroad tracks or the building of factories, and no one need physically relocate—it does require the building of pathways. And in this sense, opportunities are availing themselves to anyone who is willing to move from old to new, from the farm to the factory.

Our twenty-first-century Cottonopolis is populated by self-selected crowds and represents a modern-day version of an industrialized city to which we should relocate in order to cultivate our lives and careers. It is a city built of networks rather than timber, of relationships as opposed to concrete and steel. A digitally based megalopolis where the sociotechno revolution involves no smog or construction and no mass exodus or population shift—one in which the railways and canals are virtual, not physical.

What technology-based networking provides, in the most simplistic terms, is the ability to connect two people. Even though these connected pairs may be thousands of miles apart geographically, and in some cases a million miles apart socioeconomically or even culturally, the connection must put them in the same *emotional* space in order to be effective. The key to building effective networks is in reducing the space between people. When we reduce the space between people, one who has a need, however defined, and the other armed with a solution, we reduce the time and energy needed to solve a problem or achieve a goal.

The reason crowdsourcing allows for results of exothermic proportion is due, at least in part, to the fact that it reduces the average path length between two critical and often perfectly matched nodes.

↬

AVERAGE PATH LENGTH (APL), a graph theory component that simply measures the average length of the quickest/shortest paths or connections between pairs of nodes (endpoints or intersections) within a network, is one of the key metrics applied in the study of networks in general. While APL cannot be used to solve a problem, it can be used as a means to understand how to *approach* one. APL relates to small-world theory

... world via only six steps. This may have originally stemmed, at least somewhat, from a 1929 short story called "Chain-Links" by the Hungarian author Frigyes Karinthy, in which one of the characters bets that he can get in touch with anyone on Earth through a sequence of five or fewer people. This was evidently reflective of Karinthy's own personal belief that although the world was growing in population, it was actually becoming smaller due to advances in technology—and this was *over eighty years ago*. While a specific number (five or six) has not been definitively proven, many well-known experiments have been conducted in this regard,[38] and it is generally accepted by scientists and mathematicians that there is evidence to support this premise.

In fact, the theory is so commonly known that it moved into the pop culture space, first in the form of an award-winning play (which was later made into the movie that launched Will Smith's feature film career), and as a "party trick" in the midnineties as a game called "Six Degrees of Kevin Bacon"—the idea being that Bacon could be connected to any other actor or actress in six steps or fewer. I won't go through all of the iterations, and I'm sure everyone knows of the game, but this concept has been mathematically challenged using an algorithm that pulls from a pool

---

38. Dr. Stanley Milgram's work at Harvard University in the 1960s is an early example of this research.

of roughly one million credited actors on IMDb,[39] which is large enough that it can be used as a sample pool, and Bacon ranks in the top 1 percent in terms of Hollywood APL.[40] In fact, it is estimated that the APL between Kevin Bacon and the majority of other screen actors is less than three.

This concept of connectivity and small-world networks is significant, as it is indicative of who and what we are capable of reaching and attaining through channels that already exist in our own lives. Further, given today's tools, we can strategically expand our networks to include more nodes (target connections and relationships) and reduce APL.

Reducing APL increases opportunity. When sourcing the crowd on a personal and career-based level, the goal is to become, in a mathematical sense, Kevin Bacon.

To accomplish this we need to recognize, and then cultivate, key relationships with the facilitators in each of our respective networks.

⤳

DAN LACK HAS built a career based on creating "quality relationships" not just between himself and others but by connecting other like-minded individuals as well. Think of him as an intellectual matchmaker of sorts. A connector. One of his websites[41] features interviews with impressive leaders and thinkers "who are following their passions," and in perusing the list of well-known individuals it is easy to recognize that Dan is very good at what he does. He worked for author Keith Ferrazzi and now runs business endeavors of his own, including Pushing Beyond and producing and hosting exclusive retreats for "high-impact entrepreneurs and philanthropists" through Meeting of

---

39. Internet Movie Database.
40. Brett Tjaden created this algorithm for his website www.oracleofbacon.com.
41. http://www.pushingbeyond.com.

the Big Minds,[42] which brings together fifteen young leaders for four days to help one another become more successful. A key aspect of Dan's success in all these efforts is the way in which he values face-to-face relationships, which makes it even more interesting to observe the way in which he ~~facili~~ ...

... ~~back home~~ to Atlanta to cofound a pizza franchise, and when he considered entering the traditional corporate workforce, he knew it wasn't for him. "Back in 2009 (age twenty-four), I was pondering what I wanted to do next with my life and began reaching out to my network to see what they were up to. Many who had desk jobs were unsatisfied, while those who were following their passions seemed to love their lives," he tells me. Based on the feedback from his network and his own personal background, the answer quickly became obvious. Dan's new credo became "How can I help you?" And he started meeting people and asking them just that.

When I first met Dan, he asked me this same question and immediately connected me with a few people in his network via e-mail, purely in the interest of seeing like-minded individuals connect, and reinforcing the value of face-to-face meetings, he invited me to a dinner at his house. "There are going to be a lot of people there you should meet," Dan told me, just as Jessica Jackley had a few months earlier. The twenty or so people in attendance were all inspirational and successful young individuals, a few of whom I already knew. I was able to reconnect with some friends I hadn't seen in a while, and Dan also facilitated connections with a few people I had not met previously.

One conceptual incongruity is the belief that as we become more

---

42. http://www.meetingofthebigminds.com.

global, as we become connected with larger groups, we can become more isolated in our technology-based social spaces. When these tools are utilized correctly, however, relationships fueled by online-based networking can move to the level of face-to-face with exponential speed, either literally or by proxy. As we conduct introductions, get to know people and their ideas, and become engaged in their interests, stories, and work—through shared goals, common friends, or connective platforms—sourcing our online networks can be an accelerant to *deeper* relationship building as opposed to an isolating factor. If, and when, we finally meet face-to-face, the relationship often manifests in an exponentially more intimate manner because we have vested emotional currency in each others' stories—the relationship ties that have been established through common connections and interests create an atmosphere of trust.

> *When online-based networking is utilized strategically,*
> *it allows us to leverage our cumulative connections in a*
> *disproportionately large and exothermic manner. In*
> *other words, we need to approach personal, connectivity-*
> *based crowdsourcing as six degrees of "preparation."*

And the beauty of online networking is that we just have to ask for an introduction—not for an invitation to dinner at someone's home. Once introduced, we need to connect in a reciprocal manner to create a relationship of meaning. "Live proactively, not passively," advises Dan, who has had undeniably diverse experiences for someone his age. "Social media enhances. But real relationships, face-to-face relationships, are the most valuable because they facilitate a stronger bond and the ability to help others—which for me is the end goal," he asserts.

As if proving his own core beliefs, Dan facilitated one face-to-face meeting that ended up being particularly interesting to me. Over the past few months I had been hearing more and more about a young man named Adam Braun who had created an education initiative called

Pencils of Promise (PoP) that was becoming highly successful in using a crowdsourcing model to raise awareness and facilitate fund-raising efforts to build schools in impoverished communities around the world. At the time, plans were in development for PoP to build ~~~ schools in a number of ~~~~ ~

~~~ ~~ calculated plot" to ~~~~~~ with him through a series of seemingly coincidental circumstances—I just went over to Dan Lack's house for dinner. But as I crowdfriended my way to Adam Braun, I learned just how effectively he too was using a derivative of crowdsourcing to accomplish his own goals.

↪

DURING HIS JUNIOR year of college, in January of 2005, Adam Braun was thirteen days into a semester at sea program when the vessel was struck by a "fifty-five-foot rogue wave." Engines died, bulletproof glass shattered from the impact, and hysteria ensued. Writes Braun, "Left to the mercy of the surrounding forty-foot swells, prayer circles and screams could be heard for hours. Somehow, we miraculously survived the certain-death experience."[43] From that moment, he tells me, his perspective was forever changed.

As he was finishing his degree, Adam began backpacking whenever possible, and after graduating in 2006, unhindered by classes, he spent a complete year traveling across the world. Adam, who has visited over fifty countries, including India, Cambodia, and Bolivia, tells me from New York City a few days after our initial meeting in California that during

43. http://www.pencilsofpromise.org.

the course of his travels he made it a point to interact with individuals from as many different walks of life as possible. He would ask the local citizens why certain structures and resources weren't being utilized, and the most common response, he tells me, was "because the government or an NGO built it *for* us, not *with* us." But everything changed for Adam when he asked a small boy what he wanted more than anything in the world. The child's profoundly moving response was simply, "A pencil."

Adam, of course, gave the boy a pencil from his knapsack—and then watched as his face lit up. Adam realized through the power of this transaction, with something as simple as a pencil, he could help combat a global humanitarian issue—and perhaps fulfill some individual dreams as well. Education should be a basic human right, he reasoned, and with the cost of providing an education in developing nations a fraction of what it equates to in the United States, it is, at least from a monetary standpoint, an approachable problem. Inspired by the conversations that resulted from handing out many more pencils during his travels, and astounded at the unserved educational needs of children in certain regions of the world, he decided to take action. "I wanted to develop a for-profit skill set that could be applied in the nonprofit arena one day," he explains. With this in mind he took a job working in banking in New York City at Bain & Company, a global management-consulting firm, getting a "business background with the knowledge that I wanted to start a nonprofit organization."

Adam founded Pencils of Promise in October of 2008 with twenty-five dollars. The goal was to build one school in Pha Theung, Laos. And not just "build" a school—four walls and a roof—but a school that the local community could "take ownership of," he tells me. "I noticed a lack of connection between the people who wanted to do good versus those who were on the ground," he further explains. In essence, a facilitator was needed—a partner to connect the two groups. "My goal was to create an NPO[44] that had a sustainable effect." And PoP is providing just that.

---

44. Nonprofit organization.

The size and scope of what happened caught Braun a bit off guard. Within six months PoP had seventy-five volunteers and had generated over fifty thousand dollars in donations, mostly through no-cost viral marketing on Facebook and Twitter. "We had almost two thousand donations for the first school ~~ 1 '~~

~~..... ~~v~~ ~~ιuι~~u a project

~~.. .~~ ~~ι~~v gcι one person or entity to do the same. During that first year, PoP was able to construct three schools. In 2009, while still a relatively brand-new initiative, they raised over $125,000, with 90 percent of the donations coming from twenty-somethings, once again at an average amount of less than $100 each.[45]

"We want to work with these communities as active partners. We don't simply go in, build a structure, and leave. We tell the local leaders that they have to make this happen *with* us," Adam explains. For this reason PoP asks that each community or village contribute at least 10 percent of the construction efforts (typically in the way of material and resources as opposed to financial capital), thereby ensuring that the community is taking ownership of the project. "Ownership leads to sustainability," Adam tells me, illustrating many of PoP's "Founding Principles," which emphasize the fact that the communities are their most important partners, that the goal is to build education, not simply structures, and that they are dedicated to long-term sustainability when it comes to each project.

"Once the school is built, that's when it all starts," Adam says, which is important to note, as this juncture is typically the end of the road for most organizations. He points out that we are members of an

45. www.pencilsofpromise.org.

interconnected world and that crowdsourcing, peer-to-peer networking, and social media have been the platform that has spawned much of
PoP's success. "We've always channeled through Facebook, and of
course now with Twitter, and these are tools that can be used to sustain
a global community." Indeed, the power of the crowd—over two hundred and fifty thousand online supporters and counting as of spring
2011—is helping to carry the vision behind Pencils of Promise to
fruition.[46]

With over thirty projects nearing completion, PoP is not only helping young children receive an education in each of these communities
short term but also helping them avoid the traditional traps that face an
uneducated populace long term. Quick to highlight the importance of
education, Adam says, "No country has ever achieved rapid and con-
tinuous economic growth without first having at least forty percent of
its adults able to read and write.

"Breathe your fire, and the energy of a profound idea can become
unstoppable," Adam tells me. "These things happen slowly, and with a
lot of work." And he could be referring to just about anything in life—
not specifically starting an international NPO.

> *"Breathe your fire," he says again, "and your*
> *energy will make you unstoppable."*

↜

SUCCESSFUL INDIVIDUALS AND leaders all seem to have a keen
sense—call it a social intelligence—that leads to strategic building of

---

46. Adam Braun was named to *Wired Magazine's* 2012 Smart List of 50 People
Changing the World and to the Dell #Inspire 100 list, "a compilation of leading influencers in entrepreneurship, philanthropy, education, and media who have used
technology to empower and inspire others." He was also listed as one of the "30
Under 30: Education" list for *Forbes,* and Pencils of Promise was called "the hottest
nonprofit in the country" by ABC News.

their own crowds. They cultivate the "right" relationships and then motivate and incentivize the peers within their networks to want to help them—and they are always happy to return the favor. These are mutually beneficial relationships of *meaning*. These individuals are essentially involved in coll...

..., Kiva, ProFounder, or ...ons of Promise does. They harness metaphorical CPUs in order to generate exothermic energy.

What these stories all have in common revolves around *reach, personal engagement*, and structuring a *reasonable ask*. The Internet obviously allows us to reach much farther and a lot faster than old-fashioned networking techniques—but these connections only manifest as valuable if we create relationships of meaning. And to do that, we have to replicate in our online exchanges the same level of personal engagement usually generated in a face-to-face meeting.

KIVA reaches all the way around the globe, connecting people from faraway places, and then simulates the intimacy of a face-to-face meeting by using pictures and compelling personal stories of need. They then offer us an easy way to help, by keeping the ask small—the loan of a few dollars. They create a meaningful, *ongoing*, and rewarding connection between two partners. Reed Hastings reached all over the world as well, engaging people by offering a financial prize using a million dollars' worth of motivation to replicate the intensity of face-to-face. SETI@home did the same, allowing technology to extend its reach around the globe, then making it personal by offering us the opportunity to become part of something bigger and keeping the ask small. In fact, what they were asking for was something we weren't using—our idle CPUs.

On a smaller, individual scale, for our own career-based networks, there is no single way to do this—it will vary from situation to situation and industry to industry, even from ask to ask. But each of us has to do the same three things: reach farther, replicate the power of face-to-face encounters by engaging in a personal manner, and formulate an ask that is small enough—or motivating enough—for the recipient to actually be inclined to act upon. If we do this incrementally, we can ask for that proverbial pencil, and, just maybe, crowdfriend, crowdconnect, and crowdsource our way to a metaphorical school as we create a network of real connections of meaning rather than just lists of "friends" by using small incremental asks—perhaps just asking for career advice or an introduction to someone at a company in a field we want to work in. Perhaps the next ask is for a recommendation, a heads-up if there is a job opening, a suggestion of another avenue to pursue, knowledge of another company that is hiring, or a suggestion of a similar field that may be of interest, or yet another contact. And because our reach is now literally borderless and often instant, we can crowdfriend, crowdsurf, and crowdsource our way to something that can actually have real, tangible impact on our lives. If we start with our friends and family, expand outward to their connections, join organizations online that we actually participate in rather than just add to our lists, then we can begin to establish a network of meaning.

> *When we apply these principles to our own lives and careers, we can rapidly accelerate personal growth and opportunity—oftentimes creating opportunities we didn't know existed.*

Many of us don't realize the potential of our digitally connected Cottonopolis. In essence, we are still stuck on the farm. We have been given a powerful tool that we don't completely understand how to use, so instead of harnessing its real potential, we break off a few pieces and improvise. Just like the Bolivian villagers described by Elizabeth McKee Gore, who tore apart a tractor to build a shelter, many of us have taken the fragmented parts of new technology and used them to build temporary shelters for ourselves, while people like Jessica Jackley, Dan Jack Adam Braun and so m

While it might be fun to see how many people are following us on Twitter, or to use the tools of social networking solely to keep in touch with our peers, it isn't necessarily the most effective use of such high-tech power. We might fool ourselves by making a handful of one-dimensional, nonessential business connections—all the while *thinking* we're farming with a high-tech tool. But all we need do is look over at the next village to see what they've accomplished with this same tool and realize that it's not too late to move out of our temporary shelters, reassemble the tractor, and begin to use the resources we have been given to actually till the land and harvest something worthy of all this power.

> *Twenty-first-century success will be found, to a large degree, in the proliferation of personalized crowdsourcing; in the assembly, structure, and prescient exploitation of the exothermic power of strategically built and sourced networks.*

6

BECOMING A DISRUPTER

*Subvert Power Structures, Raze Barriers,
and Sit at the Wrong Table*

■

In a gentle way, you can shake the world.

—MOHANDAS GANDHI

B ACK IN THE early 1990s, a twenty-seven-year-old software
developer named Ron Avitzur had been working on a "secret
project" for Apple Computer[47] that was so riddled with problems it was eventually canceled. Ron was determined to finish the part
of the project he had been involved with, which was developing the
original Pacific Tech Graphing Calculator, but with the contract canceled, he found himself officially unemployed. Rather than heading
home to update his résumé and look for a new job, Ron just kept on
showing up every day to work at Apple as if nothing had changed. His
electronic access badge wasn't confiscated or deactivated, so he was still
able to get into the building. The way he figured it, the only real difference

47. The company changed its name to Apple in January 2007.

in his day-to-day situation, other than the minor technicality of having lost his job and the fact that he occasionally had to answer a few awkward questions from security or move from one vacant office to another when a "real" Apple employee showed up, was that he was no longer being paid

. . . as asked to leave and was even escorted out of the building, but he just showed up again the next day anyway. When his badge was eventually confiscated, he would simply wait outside one of the doors and "tailgate" other employees into the complex. He convinced an engineer whose contract with Apple had just finished to work alongside him on his project—also for no pay and without any corporate authority to do so—and the two of them eventually secured a couple of vendor badges through Apple (the same kind used by maintenance and repair employees), giving them relatively easy access to the offices. What they found was that without a boss to report to or meetings to attend, they were, according to Ron, "unbelievably productive."

When Ron asked himself to justify why he was "sneaking into an eight-billion-dollar corporation to do volunteer work," he said, "Apple was having financial troubles then, so we joked that we were volunteering for a nonprofit organization." He later suggested, with a little tongue-in-cheek humor, that he would have tried the same stunt and developed a version of the Graphing Calculator for Windows 98, "but sadly, Microsoft has effective building security."

Although neither Ron nor his newly recruited partner were working for Apple, either officially or unofficially, they managed to finish developing the Graphing Calculator as intended. It was an endeavor that involved many months of grueling work, from writing complicated code to testing the software. During the process they enlisted the support of a number of "real" Apple employees who had expertise in quality assurance, graphic design, and user interface—most of whom thought the whole subversive nature of the project was geek chic, or as Ron put it, "cool." There was, at the time, a particular engineer at the company who was responsible for creating what was called the "Golden Master" hard disk, which contained all of the system software that would be sent to Apple's manufacturing plant and then installed on new machines. "He told me that if I gave him our software the day before the production run began, it could appear on the Golden Master disk," Ron says. They made sure to have the software ready for him on time, and despite the odds stacked against it, with no authorization from Apple itself, the Pacific Tech Graphing Calculator was included on the Golden Master disk. Since then, Ron states, it has "been shipped on over twenty million machines."[48]

When the whole escapade was over, Ron arranged for a *New York Times* interview, which appeared on the front page of the business section along with a picture of him and his development partner. A woman from public relations at Apple contacted Ron to say that software engineers weren't permitted to speak to the press, but as Ron points out, "It's kind of hard to enforce that kind of thing with people who can't be fired."

When Ron tells the story, he makes it clear that he did all of this in part due to a genuine interest in finishing a project he believed in coupled with a real desire to help children with math. "Public schools are too poor to buy software, so the most effective way to deliver it is to install it at the factory," he states. But he also willingly admits that he did it in part to "subvert power structures." He kept working at Apple after he was let go,

---

48. Avitzur was able to eventually license the software to Apple for "a nominal fee."

he says, because he liked the freedom of working on his own terms and, as he puts it, "partly for the sheer joy of creating something."

Although this was a clandestine, admittedly subversive, corporate covert op conducted beneath the radar of the higher-ups at Apple, it is

, ... a pattern, if not in scope and detail, at least in direction, that I detected in the behavior of many of the individuals I had been speaking with and writing about. They all have a proclivity to want to shake things up, or as Ron put it, "subvert power structures."

> *Functioning as a disruptive force is, in one form*
> *or another, a natural inclination among*
> *highly successful people.*

The recent "open science movement," which aims to create transparency and provide free and easy access to medical information, not only between researchers, doctors, and patients, but among scientists from different fields as well, is a clear example of a positive disruptive force. But often when we think about disruptive forces, we think of actions and behaviors that *interfere* with productivity rather than those that enhance it—leading us to conjure up thoughts of events with the potential for enormous negativity. Perhaps what comes to mind is something akin to the building of nuclear weapons during the Manhattan Project or Operation CHAOS, in which President Lyndon Johnson engaged the CIA to disrupt Vietnam War protests and look for Soviet instigators on U.S. college campuses, or maybe a cloak-and-dagger coup d'état on foreign soil.

In the broadest sense, a disruptive force might simply be viewed as any-thing that alters productivity or changes established patterns—either for better or for worse. But when most of us think about disruptive forces, we don't think about software engineers sneaking into billion-dollar compa-nies to work for free.

When the Einstein-Szilard letter of 1939 was sent to President Franklin D. Roosevelt by Albert Einstein and Leo Szilard, warning that it would soon be possible to split the uranium atom to create a nuclear chain reaction that could generate massive explosive power with enough radioactive fallout to contaminate a sizable area for generations—the correspondence responsible for originating the Manhattan Project—presidential staffers withheld the letter for many weeks after it arrived, feeling that Roosevelt was too preoccupied with Hitler's invasion of Poland at the time to read it. A historical reminder that when thinking about disruptive forces we also have to consider the randomness of events and the sometimes blurred line that exists between the positive and the negative. In a more contemporary context we have only to look to Google's presence in (and then forced exit from) China, the emer-gence of WikiLeaks, the Stuxnet computer worm that infiltrated Iran's nuclear program, or the role that social media played in the Egyptian revolution of 2011 to see exactly how blurred that line can be.

If Ron Avitzur hadn't enlisted the cooperation of the engineer responsible for shipping the Golden Master disk, if Apple had stricter security at the time, or if his subversive behavior had caused corporate harm, his story would have had a very different outcome. And we can only begin to imagine what might have happened on a global level if Roosevelt never got the Einstein–Szilard letter back in 1939—or per-haps if its delivery had been delayed a few weeks longer—as we wait to see how the more contemporary disruptions surrounding Google, WikiLeaks, Iran, and Egypt play out. Regardless of the interplay of ran-dom chance, fortuitous or ill-fated circumstances, and the often some-what hard-to-discern difference between the good and the bad, when considering disruptive forces I specifically homed in on the more benevolent Ron Avitzur type that disrupts en route to *construct* productive results.

...through German-controlled Czechoslovakian mines, it was infinitely more disruptive than Ron Avitzur's clandestine "philanthropic" work for Apple.

Napster represents an early example of connectivity-based file sharing manifesting as a sizable disruptive force—one that served to create a paradigm shift within an industry—and one that had more than a bit of radioactive fallout of its own. Even though the free, peer-to-peer, digital-content-sharing (predominantly music) site was preemptively shut down in response to the issuing of a court order based on charges of copyright infringement—as most of us are now avid consumers of legally distributed digital content—arguably, in the case of Napster, most of that fallout was good.

Since I had been noticing a pattern among successful entrepreneurs to openly and continuously challenge existing paradigms, I decided that if Fanning managed to initiate this much disruption from his dorm room as a college student, it would be worthwhile to go speak with him about what he was currently working on, a decade after the initial incarnation of Napster was shut down. More important, I wanted to determine how the rest of us can use the concept of being a disruptive force within our own lives to subvert a little bit of power and "shake things up"—even if the resultant paradigm shift only manifests as change on a personal level.

⤺

AS SECURITY WAS escorting me to the elevator through the sprawling lobby of Shawn Fanning's luxury building in San Francisco, my mind was racing as I tried to map out potential topics for discussion. Of all the interviews and meetings I had conducted over the last several months, Fanning's story, at least as it pertains to Napster, is certainly among the most well known—even though his is not necessarily a household name.

In 1999, while a student at Northeastern University, Shawn created and founded the highly controversial company—which went on to become the largest file-sharing hub in the world during it's brief two-year existence—with business partner Sean Parker[49] and his uncle John Fanning. In Napster's original form, by signing up for the free service, it allowed other community members access to any music or other digital content stored on your computer, and you had the ability to access their content as well. The problem became instantly self-evident. There was no way for the record labels or the artists to make any money if content, in this case mainly in the form of digital music files, was widely available for free as a result of piracy.[50]

As an early execution of peer-to-peer file sharing and digital content distribution, Napster is a prime example of how enormously powerful a disruptive force can be, even if, in its original form, it was never intended to be one. Napster changed the power structure within the music industry from the standpoint of distribution and content delivery by dramatically altering the manner in which consumers could access music. It also simultaneously altered the access musicians—including

---

49. Parker went on to become the founding president of Facebook, cofounder of Causes, and is a partner at the Founders Fund.
50. Readers old enough to have used Napster may recall their own concerns about the possibility of having their computers confiscated for downloading music in their dorm rooms.

independent artists—had to potential fans, thus rupturing what was a
well-established system in which record labels, by and large, controlled
content.

The overwhelming popularity and controversial nature of Napster

_, _____ _, ... ___._, as did hearings before Congress,
spawning eventual injunctions to attempt to shut down what had
become a global online community in excess of twenty million people.
After multiple legal battles, copyright-infringement complaints, and
a failed attempt by Napster to successfully comply with court orders,
it was taken off-line voluntarily. Not long after, Napster filed for Chapter 11 bankruptcy and was eventually sold and relaunched as a pay
service.

This boom-to-bust story illustrates how Napster became a highly
disruptive force that changed the way we consume music and protect
digital versions of copyrighted material, and also how it forced the
industry as a whole, in an inadvertently productive way, to modernize
by realigning itself with emerging technology. As evidenced in the subsequent massive success of pay services like iTunes, it sent out concen-
tric waves of change that would create a domino effect in terms of how
we consume, distribute, monetize, and legally regulate all forms of

51. Napster is largely credited with helping Radiohead crack the Top 20 on the *Billboard* charts for the first time in their career when *Kid A* debuted at No. 1, for example, because the album had been leaked on Napster prior to its official release. In
some cases, Napster actually functioned to increase music sales by providing artists
a larger pool of potential consumers who were introduced to music via free download, and would then purchase albums, concert tickets, and merchandise.

copyrighted digitized content as it becomes available in television, film, books, and other print media.

Knowing full well how disruptive a force Fanning could be, as evidenced by what is clearly a natural proclivity to seek out disruptive opportunities, I was interested to learn about some of his newer projects. And this is where I ran into a problem. After Napster, Shawn went on to become involved with a number of well-known endeavors, including the music platform SNOCAP and a gaming-based social networking hub called Rupture, the latter of which was acquired by Electronic Arts for a reported fifteen million dollars. But for the previous year or so, Fanning's projects, most visibly Path, had been a bit secretive as they were being developed (Path launched as a photo-sharing mobile application after our interview). At the time, however, the Path website gave no indication as to *what* it actually was. Rather, it presented as a simple landing page. Because the founders were Shawn, former Facebook senior platform manager Dave Morin, and Macster cofounder Dustin Mierau, my interest was certainly piqued. So, having no real concrete questions or any idea as to which direction our conversation might lead, and a lack of information as to what he was working on at the time, I entered the elevator and began my ascent to one of the building's top floors. Feeling appropriately unprepared, I was able to default to one of my favorite interview strategies—I stepped back to see what Shawn wanted to talk about.

～

A YOUNG WOMAN who couldn't have been more than a few years out of college greets me at the door and leads me through a deceptively large office with a completely wide-open workspace. Roughly eight to ten young professionals and programmers are working away on Macs as we navigate our way through a fully-stocked kitchen, a meeting room, a dining area, and then into a massive corner office that appears to also double as Shawn's bedroom. The view is expansive, revealing a completely clear panorama overlooking the bay. Two musicians are working with Shawn on a drumbeat as I notice that the room is also a recording studio complete with instruments and turntables, as well as a plethora

...to only people. Clearly, one of the most interesting issues surrounding new technology and online communities is not only when and how to appropriately size our personal networks, but what to share with them as well. Path is uniquely designed to provide a platform for sharing photos with a smaller, more intimate group of friends and family than we typically would through other social networking sites or applications.

When I ask Shawn about the aforementioned social-gaming endeavor Rupture, and gaming in general, which he tells me is of huge personal interest—as I can clearly see by the impressive stacks of video games and accessories surrounding his flat screen—I find his response to be quite intriguing. "Game mechanics are fascinating, especially if you can use them in a way to enhance people's lives, to 'trick' them into doing the things they need to do," Shawn tells me. What most people may see as a "game," Shawn sees as an opportunity to disrupt—in this case by using game mechanics to undertake complex psychological manipulation to, as he puts it, "enhance people's lives."

"One of the tech projects I'm working on right now," Shawn tells me, "is all about meeting new people. Which is incredibly complicated because of the social dynamics of reaching out to someone—your social value drops, maybe they're suspicious. If you approach someone on the street randomly, there's this built-in anxiety," he explains. "It's like evolutionary psychology, these built-in inhibitions we have. There's a lot of related stuff that comes into play, but you come up with a theory and then you test it. If you're right, great. If you're wrong, then you know what to test next. And you just kind of go with it. And you're just building up a foundation.

"I do a lot of work with entrepreneurs," Shawn goes on to say. "I often tell them the things that they don't want to hear, that no one else will tell them. But that's what I'm here for." He is referencing his own ability to function as a disruptive force by analyzing and offering advice from a different perspective than that of someone who has been entrenched in the same confined vertical space for an extended period of time. "In terms of personalities, I like to work with people who don't really see boundaries," he says. "You know that they consistently seem to succeed, but you're not quite sure why." What I am thinking when Shawn says this, of course, is that he recognizes the value in the collective power of aligning himself with other like-minded, disruptive forces—people who, as he puts it, "Aren't afraid to think big."

Shawn is vested in several other businesses in addition to Path, either as an investor or consultant, including BranchOut, a career-based connectivity application similar to LinkedIn but conveniently designed to run through Facebook, which allows users to exponentially expand access to potential employers, and Diversion, a gaming company where he sits on the board with Michael Eisner, who served as the CEO of The Walt Disney Company for over twenty years. Our conversation darts from topic to topic at first, but largely revolves around making the right decisions at the right time in one's life. In Shawn's case, when to pursue certain projects of interest over others, when to accept certain offers, when to sell, whom to work with, and what it means to fail. And virtually every one of these observations revolves around his natural instinct to "shake things up" by subverting power within industries, within companies, and within his own life.

But what Shawn really wants to talk about, what he keeps going back to in our conversation, isn't Path, Rupture, Diversion, BranchOut, or any of the other endeavors he is working on or has invested in. Instead, Shawn wants to tell me about a pet project of his that tracks

. . . . y glides across the room in his office chair to grab a massive black duffel bag. He rolls back, opening the bag to reveal dozens of bottles of natural organic supplements and starts asking questions about what I had eaten that day (cereal and a Caesar salad), and how much I had been traveling lately (a lot). He asks whether I had recently changed time zones (yes), how much sleep I had gotten in the previous forty-eight hours (not much), whether or not I had any coffee that morning (yes, again), along with a slew of other questions. And even though I know I am getting a truncated version of the full project, which I instantly realize as he briefly references some of the data he has been collecting from his other subjects, himself included, I can see how vested he is in its development.

"Okay, I'm just figuring out what your regimen would look like," he says quietly. After a few minutes he explains what he recommends and why, then reassures me that these are all natural supplements you can get at your local health food store: some B_{12}, vitamin C, zinc, and an organic metabolism booster, among others. I'm familiar with most of these supplements, and I swallow all ten of the pills. Then Shawn brings me into the kitchen, quietly and confidently firing off answers to questions from members of his staff about coding and analytics along the way, and takes a blender out of the cupboard. "Do you want me to make you an amazing organic cleansing drink?" he asks me energetically. I'm surprised that this is what seems to interest Shawn more than anything else that is happening around him, which includes a company-wide meeting about a tech endeavor and an ongoing series of seemingly important business decisions.

"I do this program for about sixty-five of my friends and family, and I've been messing around with the data," Shawn tells me as he puts a variety of fruits, vegetables, and powders into the blender. "It's great. I've helped people get off of heavy medication for depression and attention deficit disorder, quit smoking, and increase their overall quality of life through the use of natural supplements and nutrients. I look at the data points and I realize that I need to have less sleep, for example. This program has helped the quality of my sleep, it's helped my brain function, and the reason I understand how all this stuff works is because of my background in computer programming. It's sort of the same thing." As I drink the greenish-brown smoothie he had whipped up for me, I think once again about the potential value of being a disruptive force when approaching problems or challenges, taken by the fact that Shawn had just told me that nutritional healing is the same as computer programming, and prior to that he mentioned that game mechanics can be used to modify human behavior for positive life change.

"I want to have everything monitored, so that I can actually do it more scientifically, integrate it, and then track everything I consume," Shawn tells me as we sit back down. "It helps people. It solves a problem," he says. "Why can't I just wake up every day and know what I need? As a performance engineer, you look at it and just want to solve the problem—all the technology is there, but it's just not combined. I'm tracking and adjusting my intake based on my lifestyle.

"It's hard to explain to people because it seems too good to be true," Shawn confesses. "Health issues, food disorders, just general happiness— a lot of creative solutions come from cross-disciplinary experiences. I enjoy being able to work with a group in order to problem solve. For me, when you're doing it right, these things choose you. I have no control over it," he says. "It works, and I just have to do something about it. I see that I have the ability to fix a problem, so it becomes challenging to *not* talk to everyone I know about it. It's a longer-term goal, and it's fun. It's like root cause analysis," is

[text obscured] he responds, when asked if this is something he would consider developing as a business. Shawn is conscious of the potential misconceptions that might arise if he were to launch such an endeavor to the public, no matter how good the intentions. "If you don't have some way of limiting that 'consumer defense mechanism,' it's not going to work," he tells me. "There's no way to convey to people that this stuff works as well as it does without sounding like you're selling them something, you know? Especially with someone like me. It's like, here we go again!" he says, laughing.

Later that evening, at roughly 11:30 p.m., I get a text message from Shawn asking how I am feeling. As I respond to him that I feel great, I realize that even if this nutrition project turns out to be implemented only in his own life and the lives of a few friends and family, he is still functioning as a productive disruptive force—just on a much smaller level than he did on some of his other projects.

Shawn's strength lies in his ability to see things differently. And how this manifests is in the disruption of established paradigms. He creates new opportunities by disrupting old models. He disrupts en route to *construct* almost as a natural offshoot of how he sees things and thinks. Whether his inclination to disrupt manifests on a large scale as it did in the case of Napster or Rupture, or on the smaller scale of nutritional experimentation within his peer network, he uses it to create both opportunity and productive change.[52]

> *Acting as a disruptive force doesn't necessitate*
> *that it be on the industry-changing level of Napster.*
> *We can be disrupters in our own lives and the lives of*
> *those around us by simply applying these larger*
> *principles on a smaller, more personal level.*

⤳

AS I LEFT our meeting, I considered the fact that most people don't have the capacity to operate as a disruptive force along the lines of a Shawn Fanning, since the level of intellectual function necessary to do so may very well be beyond most of us. People like Shawn are visionary in the sense that they have what appears to be a natural talent for taking things apart and putting them back together again—with a few major adjustments. Whether accepted intellectual constructs, established business models, or simple aspects of daily life in general, disrupters on this level have the ability to institute and accelerate change on a monumental scale.

I thought back to Ron Avitzur and the psychological mind-set of dismissing convention and plowing forward headfirst with blinders on in order to accomplish a task—to "think big," just like those "people who don't really see boundaries," as Shawn so aptly put it. Then I began to think about the engineer who had control over the Golden Master disk at Apple, the presidential staffers in the FDR administration who decided to withhold the letter with information of potentially dire consequence, and the fact that hindrances or gates such as these underscore the critical role played by random variables in our lives that are completely beyond our control. When I began to integrate the impact

52. In 2012 Shawn Fanning partnered with Sean Parker to launch a video chat site called Airtime.

of a forge-ahead attitude and the effect that these random events can have on our lives, it became clear that it isn't always necessary to be a visionary thinker like Fanning in order to become a disruptive force.

Rather, it is the ability to raze established barriers and recognize and manage obstructions ~~by int~~ ...

~~... be able to see the~~ potential in these events and respond to them by adjusting our behavior to take into account each new and potential opportunity to disrupt.

Being a disruptive force on a personal scale
simply requires adaptive thinking on a level
that shouldn't be beyond any of us.

∽

MICHAEL RITTER HAS always liked communications. In high school he wanted to work for more than just his school newspaper, so he wrote personal letters to the editors of fifty magazines. Two wrote back. One was *Seventeen* and the other was the "kids'" version of the *Wall Street Journal*, as he puts it. "I got on the teen board for *Seventeen* and I really enjoyed it—I did basic stuff like checking quotes and fact finding," Ritter tells me. As a result of his position at *Seventeen* and his age, *Newsweek* contacted him to do an article called "What Teens Believe." "They picked four people from the *Seventeen* teen board and visited our high schools to do a broader interview and a photo shoot, so in 2001 I was on the cover of *Newsweek* at seventeen or eighteen years old," he adds casually.

Admittedly, he didn't necessarily intend to build a career in print magazines. "I purely did it as something fun to do," says Ritter, who launched *Saturday Night Magazine* from his dorm room while he was an undergraduate student at the University of Southern California (USC) in 2003–2004 after the campus newspaper failed to respond to his application requesting a position. Despite his age, Ritter has now been a magazine publisher for the better part of a decade. Like most young entrepreneurs I had been meeting with, he isn't wearing a suit and tie, and as we sit in his fourteenth-floor office around the corner from Avenue of the Stars, we begin to discuss the origins and growth of his publication.

"I'm from Los Angeles," he tells me, closing his laptop and reclining in his chair, "and a lot of my friends who moved here for school were always wondering what there was to do around town. Where to eat? Where to go on a date? Advice about the city." Recognizing the need for a service that catered to people just like his friends, specifically USC students, at least to start—Ritter founded *Saturday Night Magazine* shortly thereafter.

"We gave away all of our advertising for free for the first issue," Ritter tells me. "We had Matt Leinart on the cover, who had just won the Rose Bowl for USC. The same week we launched, he [Leinart] was also on the cover of *Sports Illustrated*, so we beat them to the punch, which was kind of cool. We set up an autograph signing on campus, which included the school president sending out his assistant to get an autograph and [then USC standout and future NFL superstar] Reggie Bush showing up. It generated enough buzz that people got really excited, including advertisers, and I was able to start paying for the next issue," he tells me. Ritter ruffled a few feathers in the process, and was even contacted by then USC football coach Pete Carroll regarding Leinart's interview (in the article, the quarterback had mentioned urinating in the pants of his gold-colored uniform during games when he couldn't make it to the locker room). Leinart would go on to win the Heisman Trophy as the best player in college football that same season, only further adding to the "heat" of what Ritter had crafted in his first issue.

"I'm a little unique in the sense that I never raised any money, had no investors, and did it myself. Literally with fifty dollars, and some credit on the first issues, I was able to start the company," Ritter tells me. "I love how start-ups say they are 'bootstrapped' when they have raised two million, or five million dollars. That's not bootstrapped. Fifty dollars is bootstrapped. Early on we would pay kids in beer to dis-

Despite the excitement around his first few issues, Ritter was still unsure as to what he wanted to pursue after college. "When I was about to graduate, I had to decide what I was going to do—which way to go. I wasn't sure if I was going to go to law school, get a job, or continue with the magazine," he tells me, sharing a sentiment that many of us can identify with in one way or another, even if the specifics of our choices are of a different nature. Before making any decisions, Ritter decided to fly to a young publishers' convention in Chicago. "It cost a few thousand dollars, which was a *lot* of money, especially for a college student, but I wanted to see if I liked being a part of that industry and if I could see myself doing what they were doing," he explains. "Turns out, I was about ten years younger than the next youngest person at the conference."

On the first day of the conference, there were a variety of dinners that attendees could sign up for. One was a dinner geared specifically toward start-up publications, and Ritter recognized a name on the list, so he registered for a seat at that table. After all, with *Saturday Night Magazine* a fledgling start-up, and knowing one of the other attendees, he figured he would be in his comfort zone.

"When I showed up for dinner I didn't really know where I was going, and someone pointed me to a table with six guys in suits," Ritter recalls. "So, I sat down with these guys and we started talking. At one

point, someone ordered food for the entire table—lobster, crab, steaks, drinks—and I'm looking around and thinking that this is going to get really expensive. Then, I start realizing that the conversation at the table has nothing to do with start-ups *at all*. The discussion revolved around expanding their reach to places like Switzerland." It quickly began to register that something clearly wasn't quite right.

"They were talking about buying and selling magazines for hundreds of millions of dollars and how to expand their global reach, and then I looked through a door in the back room and there was a table of about twenty people, one of whom I recognized. It was then that I realized I was sitting at the *wrong table*," Ritter tells me. "I literally called my dad from the bathroom and said, 'Dad, I'm at the wrong dinner table, I don't know what to do.' And I wasn't just sitting there listening, either. I was engaging with these guys and involved in the conversation. But it was too late. Dinner was being served," he says. "And then desert came, then cigars," he recounts, laughing. "Finally one of them leaned toward me during desert and asked, 'By the way, who invited you?' At first I tried playing it off," he tells me, letting everyone at the table assume that someone *else* at the table had invited him. "But the jig was up. No one at the table knew me.

"And so, I announced to everyone," Ritter says, still acknowledging the relative absurdity of the situation even years later, "'I think I sat at the wrong table. I'm really sorry. I'll gladly pay for myself.' And they said, 'No, no, we loved having you at the table.' Each of them ended up coming to my presentation the next day, and out of that dinner I developed relationships with two people who are on my board of advisers to this very day. I had an absolute blast, and I realized that night that I wanted to be a publisher," he tells me. "It was one of those life-altering moments. I thought, 'This is what I want to do, because I want to be like these guys,' and I got to peer into their world. They treated me like an equal. I can point to the exact reason I am in this industry and where I am today, and it is because I sat at the wrong table for an entire dinner."

Michael Ritter, like so many successful people, converts obstacles and barriers into opportunity. He effectively acts as a disruptive force in his own life in the way he responds to events. He did this first by starting his own magazine when his college newspaper ignored him, and then again when h~~~~~~

~~~~~ ~~~~~~~~~~

things and talk to people, because you never know what could happen. You talk to the wrong person by accident, and look at what happens. That's the value of face-to-face."

By intentionally sitting at the "wrong table," by forcing ourselves to interact with people and networks outside of our comfort zones, we can become disruptive forces in our own lives and create opportunity.

Several years and dozens upon dozens of issues later, *Saturday Night Magazine* boasts a readership of over 250,000 in the eighteen-to-twenty-nine demographic and is circulated for free up and down the West Coast. They generate their revenue through brand-name advertisers—which include Budweiser and the U.S. Army—rather than by selling issues at newsstands or via subscription. At the time we spoke, there were about twenty people who worked on the magazine, which included a combination of freelance and full-time employees. "We have a very well-developed internship program that is designed to generate real experience, including college credit. We want to help people learn to be hands-on, to help them get printed in the magazine so they get a byline, and then help place them at larger companies if that's what they want,"

Ritter says. "We've had former interns get placed at *Glamour* and *US Weekly*," he proudly tells me.

But Ritter wasn't just operating as a disruptive force in his own life, he was acting as a disruptive force within the highly competitive print media industry as well. "I always wanted to have celebrities on the cover, and I always wanted to feature young people because of our audience. I wanted to make sure that we were developing content on our own, and that was always really important for the quality of the publication. We found that by contacting 'middle level' celebrities, who were on the cusp of becoming household names, we were able to compete," he explains. "Everyone knows who Jennifer Aniston is, and she's on the cover of every magazine, which goes back to the competition aspect. *US Weekly* is going to get a better interview and more access than we are." Ritter had found his niche. From there, it simply became a question of execution.

Celebrities who graced the cover of *Saturday Night Magazine* while still on their way up include Jessica Alba, Rachel Bilson, Scarlett Johansson, Katy Perry, Kristen Bell, and Sophia Bush, to name a few. They also got their fair share of celebrities who were already established, including Katie Couric, the late DJ AM, and many others. "We did a photo shoot with Jack Black at the Four Seasons," recalls Ritter, "and the photographer forgot the white sheet for the background, so we took the sheets off the bed to use as the backdrop for the photo shoot." The magazine also featured an exclusive interview with Laura Ling right before she went on her trip to South Korea for (Al Gore's) Current TV. "A few weeks later she was in a North Korean prison," he says. Even though they are a relatively small publication whose distribution is almost exclusively on the West Coast, Ritter and his team always seem to be onto the next big thing *before* it's the next big thing.

"Our audience is more likely to be interested in the fun side-character on the show or in a movie," muses Ritter, "so we fell into the niche of working with these people. What's great is we get a full day with them—photo shoots, interviews—and they're more candid with us because they are excited to be in a magazine. For many of them, it's their first cover. So, on that level, we can compete." Ritter found a way to thrive by competing in a space in which he could "win." The larger concept of disrupting, manifesting here on a micro level, has proven to be a beneficial means to an end

...... ability to dis-

...... is perhaps even more valuable. "The personal touch is really being lost as we [as a society] go more and more digital. That's why we're sure to take a picture of me and our cover models together for each issue—it legitimizes us to our readers and our advertisers," he explains. "This isn't just some recycled story."

Ritter's approach to getting interviews and great cover stories can be applied by anyone seeking something bigger for themselves, whether it be a job, a new opportunity, career advice, or connecting with a person we feel might be able to help us. "You can't always just call and ask for it, because you won't get it. You have to entice people to want to call you," he says matter-of-factly. "So we send our magazines out to all the publicists and studios in town, we send personalized letters, and we see who comes back to us." A consistently successful yet surprisingly untraditional approach in the modern age to be sure, where most of us fire off fifty "canned" e-mails or letters on a fairly regular basis. Ritter is proving that nontraditional and perhaps even counterintuitive action can result in found opportunity.[53]

---

53. Elizabeth McKee Gore commented to me how much she values handwritten notes from job candidates, for example, and how those notes always end up at the top of her mail pile.

"We had to be very competitive, and that's the best way to describe our growth between then and now. We're an independent company, but we try to compete with national magazines like *Maxim*. We realize that we can't compete on the level of circulation or in terms of platform, but reaching a core niche audience, and doing it very well, is a platform that we can compete on," Ritter tells me, "particularly when we are flexible and can deliver a good product. You've got to get out there. I'm the only publisher I know of in terms of independent college magazines who was going out and meeting with media buyers. Geico, for example. I was the only one who was flying out to meet with the media buyer. That's why I go to a lot of conventions, trade shows, and conferences—because if you're not going to market yourself, no one is going to do it for you. If you do it aggressively and efficiently, and if you have a good product, you can be successful, even without having huge backing dollars," he says.

"I had the luxury of no overhead because I was still in college, so I got kind of lucky in that respect. There is definitely a barrier to entry, but it's not as big anymore. There are ways to be successful. You don't have to raise millions of dollars to build a business. You have to be creative, you have to be flexible, and you have to keep on going," he tells me. "The core print product is something that sets us apart from a lot of our competitors, because we have a tangible product when a lot of people are moving to the online, digital realm. We're delivering something of value, and people want that."

Several months after our interview, Ritter sent me an e-mail with an interesting update—although the terms of the deal were undisclosed at the time, a large media company had acquired *Saturday Night Magazine*. All because he razed established barriers and acted as a disrupter on his own behalf.

Maximizing our possibilities to their fullest potential by acting as a disruptive force can often lead to success that is greater than what we ever intended or imagined.

OFTEN THE BEST way to be a disrupter is to do exactly what Ron Avitzur and Michael Ritter did. When they were turned away from the jobs they wanted, they went out and

ever, they both saw an opportunity to disrupt when they recognized and managed obstructions by reframing them in an advantageous manner.

> *The ability to disrupt, to shake things up and divert a little power in our own direction, can become our biggest strength—the catalyst that propels us toward success. And to do this, to become a disruptive force in our own lives, simply requires thinking a little bit more like Shawn Fanning, Ron Avitzur, or Michael Ritter.*

7

CULTIVATING THE TWENTY-FIRST-CENTURY POLYMATH

*Accelerate Possibilities, Incubate Ideas, and
Embrace the Landscape of a Renaissance*

■

> It had long since come to my attention that people
> of accomplishment rarely sat back and let things
> happen to them. They went out and happened to
> things.
>
> —LEONARDO DA VINCI

I N 1435, IN his book entitled *Della pittura (On Painting)*, Leon Battista Alberti outlined what was, at the time, a radical concept. The first component of his breakthrough treatise was the precept that rather than painting a picture from the point of view of a heavenly figure gazing down from above (which was the common practice at the time), a scene could, in fact, be depicted from the visual perspective of the artist himself. The second and even more critical observation in his work was the concept that in painting and drawing, objects in the distance should diminish in size and recede into the background in a mathematically precise way. What Leon Battista Alberti espoused on the pages of his book introduced linear perspective to the fifteenth-century art world.

Alberti's work, if not his name, is now universally well known, but in 1435 it denoted a stunning

objects—one that accurately mirrors real-world size and proportion in relation to the relative distance between the artist (or viewer) and each of the objects depicted. *Della pittura* contains the exacting diagrams and specific instructions that are still used today to teach linear perspective to art students around the world.

What is odd about Alberti's revelation is the fact that even though we *see* with linear perspective every time we open our eyes, it is a perceptually complex enough concept that it actually required "discovery." While linear perspective represents a visual concept that may seem like it should be plainly obvious to us, here we are almost six hundred years later and it *still* needs to be taught. While we all may know that objects in the distance look proportionately smaller than objects in the foreground, all we have to do is look at a child's drawing or at a pre-Renaissance painting, in which the images generally float on a two-dimensional plane—lacking any linear perspective whatsoever—and it becomes evident that despite the fact that linear perspective is a visual "truth," most people still can't "see it" without formal instruction.

I started to frame the route to success in precisely the same terms, realizing that while the pathway to success seems like it should be obvious and easy to identify, just like linear perspective, for many of us it still needs to be taught and learned. Then I started to think more about the great innovators like Alberti and Leonardo da Vinci—polymaths who possessed high levels of knowledge spanning many areas of focus—and the explosive intellectual and artistic growth during the Renaissance, which in turn got me thinking about the conditions that incubate massive, Renaissance-like change. And it was not a coincidence that these ideas were running through my mind as I was driving down the 405 Freeway on my way to spend a day with Rafe Furst.

As I inched along the highway in bumper-to-bumper traffic toward Rafe's house and office in Santa Monica, California, I had plenty of time to think. The temperature was record breaking—approaching 115 degrees—and if my car didn't overheat, I was about to spend the bulk of the day shadowing Rafe and his team. Since Rafe is involved with so many endeavors—and given what I knew about his diverse background, I expected that the topics of our conversation were going to be changing on the fly—I have to confess that I was a bit nervous about being able to keep up.

Stephen J. Dubner of *Freakonomics* fame has cited Furst's brilliance on more than one occasion, at one point commenting on Furst's thoughts in regard to "truth markets," which he described in an e-mail to Dubner in 2006 as the concept of creating value markets in publicly administered or self-policed online communities (such as Wikipedia or Digg) in which incorrect content can be passed off as fact. What Dubner and Furst were discussing was, essentially, that without a method of ascertaining who was posting information and how reliable a source they might be, there is no way to judge the accuracy of unvetted content that is being presented as fact.

Any inaccurate data or biased information can then begin to skew disproportionately out of what is called groupthink—a concept that illustrates how the wrong answers, results, or conclusions can be reached by any "confined" group. The crowd simply "goes along with" the proponents of a particular viewpoint due to a combination of variables inherent within the dynamics of any given group. This includes the possibility that the

initial premise was based on flawed "facts," as well as restricted access to
new ideas and pressure toward uniformity. Despite the fact that Wikipedia's name implies that it is an encyclopedia, and it has taken on the authority of one, anyone can submit an entry—which may either be completely
factual or inherently flawed ...

ence or irrefutable truth. Centuries later we are still facing what amount
to be parallel issues of scribal error and the challenges of assigning *value*
to "truth." Although it wasn't framed as such, they were essentially discussing a modern-day manifestation of a fifteenth-century issue. Dubner
had specifically discussed the issue of truth value in online information
markets with Furst at the Roshambo (aka Rock-Paper-Scissors) World
Championship, and Furst followed up with an e-mail that I couldn't get
out of my head as I was driving to our meeting that day.

> ... My approach to improve Wikipedia would be to include an
> "information liquidity" metric along with each page, similar to a
> stock's trading volume. Pages could be grey-scale coded based on
> the page change history, with high-volume pages appearing
> darker, more solid. Of course this can be gamed, but here gaming
> has visible artifacts. As far as accuracy goes, I think this would
> solve Stephen's objection because the informational backwaters—
> pages with lower liquidity—would appear visually distinct from

54. Wikipedia has done a lot to improve the veracity of its entries since 2006, when
Rafe explained his theoretical model.

the heavily modified. In machine learning there's a construct called a Boltzmann Machine (aka simulated annealing machine) which describes the dynamics of systems like Wikipedia, but it requires a metric like volume/liquidity/energy . . . When coming up with the concept for truth markets, I originally was looking to create an "information reputation authority" based on the Device Reputation Authority model. I was unable though to get the model to work because of the trust bootstrap issue. Earlier incarnations of truth markets suffered from the same fate, at least in theory. The fatal argument was essentially, with no agreed-upon underlying value, what's to keep truth claims from becoming tulips? . . . I modified the model to have a quasi-external "authority" to arbitrate truth claims. The interesting thing is that the expiration date for current truth claims is a statistical distribution rather than a hard and fast date. Namely, when you trade a truth claim, all you know is that at some point in the future the issue will be voted on by a random sample of the entire market (there are mechanisms for obviating collusion or any sort of coordinated cheating). My hope is that the uncertainty of exact judgment date is enough to make individual traders act rationally with respect to their wallets at all points in time and thus coordinate price with actual truth value at all times and mitigate bubbles.[55]

In reading this e-mail, if you take away nothing else, which is very well possible, it is clear that Furst is extremely smart—no doubt falling more than a few standard deviations north of "normal" on a Gaussian curve of virtually any measure of intelligence. He holds an MS in computer science and a BS in symbolic systems from Stanford University

55. Stephen J. Dubner, comment on Furst, "Freakonomics" (blog), Oct. 25, 2006, http://www.freakonomics.com/2006/10/25/an-interesting-new-prediction-market/.

and worked for the Kestrel Institute, a major nonprofit think tank that explores "formal and knowledge-based methods for incremental automation of the software process"[56] in the early 1990s, where he got to see the early incarnations of Xmosaic, the first commonly used Web browser. He soon left Kestrel and launch

..., power

..., and more. He refers to himself officially as a "Possibility Accelerator"—someone who has the ability to propel potentially brilliant concepts into action. In essence, he is the epitome of a modern-day Renaissance man—a twenty-first-century polymath who possesses a high level of knowledge spanning many areas of focus.

In thinking about Furst's e-mail to Dubner, scribal error, the invention of the printing press and its importance in the advances made during the Renaissance, I began to consider the parallel advances occurring today that have exponentially expanded both broad and unrestricted access to information. In fact, if we compare the magnitude of the technological progress of the last decade to the impact of the fifteenth-century printing press, considering, for example, that we now consume written text in megabytes and not in scribal characters, one is almost forced to wonder if we have set the stage for a new era of Renaissance-like change based *solely* on the expansive increase in the access we now have to information.

I then began to consider that many of the people I had been interviewing for this book are in fact this generation's version of Renaissance thinkers—the polymaths of the twenty-first century who will be

56. http://www.kestrel.edu.

responsible for instigating unprecedented change. But the specific reason that I saw a connection between Alberti and Furst was that in order to understand linear perspective, Alberti applied mathematical principles to other areas of focus. By breaking through bounded thought and allowing for significant intellectual crosscurrent and the application of freewheeling thinking, he looked at the techniques used in drawing and painting from the standpoint of a mathematician rather than that of an artist. In taking this multidisciplinary approach, Alberti unhinged the art world. Similarly, Rafe Furst is applying his background in complex adaptive systems to a variety of diverse fields. And this got me thinking about the enormous value of a multidisciplinary approach to problem solving and intellectual growth, which, in turn, got me thinking even more about the Renaissance thinkers and modern-day polymaths. This then led me to scrutinize and examine the conditions that must preexist for there to be massive and fundamental change, and to consider whether or not we are standing in the foothills of another Renaissance right now.

The Renaissance scholars used their revived interest in the great philosophic works that had become widely available as a result of the invention of the printing press as an accelerant for learning, and they also employed, as a significant source of information, the knowledge gleaned from a new-found fascination with hands-on, personal exploration of their natural environment. A multidisciplinary focus and piqued curiosity surrounding nature, philosophy, science, and the arts often proved to be incongruently and *productively* distracting. For example, Leonardo da Vinci, although he painted the *Mona Lisa* and *The Last Supper*, could barely complete a project; he's attributed with only a handful of finished paintings. His time was spent pursuing a wide spectrum of interests—in particular the study of water, engineering, and aerodynamics—while his fascination with anatomy and dissecting corpses provided a foundation for his legacy of work that included his famed notebooks. (In the 1980s, Bill Gates purchased one of Leonardo's notebooks, called the "Codex Leicester," for thirty million dollars.)

As I headed to spend the day with Rafe Furst, contemplating the value of a multidisciplinary approach, I

incubating a twenty-first-century crop of polymaths.

If current conditions are set to nurture great change, it is worth noting that the biggest change is often the result of the collective achievements of many individuals. In other words, even though the Renaissance manifested historically as a macro event, it actually occurred at the time as thousands of micro events. If we are in an environment that fosters exponential Renaissance-like change, then basic logic dictates that there must be at least a few modern-day polymaths building metaphorical bridges to Constantinople and sketching brilliant diagrams of the significance and magnitude of Leonardo's *Canons of Proportion* on a white board, a piece of recycled paper, or a digital notepad.

> *Due to the expansive growth of technology and increased access to information, a virtually unending set of possible career permutations may be available to those who choose to combine unique interests and skill sets across a horizontal plane en route to crafting a polymath life.*

More important, this approach can be implemented at a variety of entry points. We don't need to view our lives and careers from a singularly focused, monomath perspective, and we don't need to be a

Leonardo da Vinci or a Rafe Furst in order to position ourselves in this manner. But what was throwing me for the biggest loop as I parked my car and made my way over to Rafe's, other than the possibility of being left in his intellectual dust, was trying to juxtapose his business acumen and high intellect with what is the overarching theme connecting virtually all of the individual components of his adult life.

⤳

POKER IS, TO a large degree, about calculating mathematical odds— and Rafe Furst certainly has the background to do that. Applying his analytical skills to poker, he has been successfully competing against some of the top competitors in the world for roughly two decades. He not only employs this background to his advantage in calculating straight mathematical odds, but he has also fostered a deep understanding of the game by applying these same analytical skills to quantify the *psychological* components that impact game strategy. Illustrating the depth to which he employs this general practice, Furst competes on the international level in Roshambo, which is actually more of a strategically played psychological mind game than one of random mathematical odds. What most perceive to be a game with a one-in-three chance of win, lose, or tie is actually a game of skill and strategy encumbered with surprisingly complex mathematical implications. For example, rock is thrown with higher frequency simply due to its perceived strength, and telling your opponent what you will throw beforehand—regardless of truth—cripples any simple probability outcome predictions by introducing another independent variable to the equation, which, as a result, radically changes the statistical dynamics. Considering the high-level approach Furst takes when playing what, to most, is a children's game, one can begin to extrapolate the underlying implications this type of thinking could bring to the far more complex game of poker, let alone the potential implications when applied to long-term, multifaceted business and life endeavors.

In 2006, Rafe won a World Series of Poker Bracelet, earning himself a spot among the most exclusive club in professional poker. For those who don't know, an official champion's bracelet is given to the winner of each event held at the World Series of Poker (WSOP) each year, and it is considered to be the greatest b~~~~ ~f ~

started while he was a student in 1989 and includes close friend and poker superstar Phil Gordon, among others), he is working on things far more important than poker. "I'd say it occupies ten percent or less of my time," Rafe tells me, which is interesting because it seems to be the catalyst that has created, inspired, and sustained many of the opportunities and relationships in his life. And in the big-idea marketplace, it seems he is always playing several hands at once. After spending the morning shadowing Rafe during various meetings and Skype calls— right after lunch and before we get to finish our conversation about the multiple projects in which he is currently involved—he hands me a pair of Oakleys and leads me onto the sun-drenched rooftop of his penthouse apartment in order to make sure that he gets some sun. Rafe Furst needs more vitamin D.

Rafe and a few close friends initially measured their vitamin D levels for health reasons, but once they received the results, they turned it into a bet. It turns out that Rafe is out on the sundeck not only for his health—he literally has money riding on the outcome. This, I learned, is not uncommon for Rafe, who, it is well chronicled, will make a wager on just about anything if he can get the right odds. To him, this type of wager is just like any other calculated investment. This particular bet involves Rafe raising his vitamin D levels by roughly 25 percent, as his test results indicated that he was below the suggested healthy amount.

Knowing that he can control the outcome based on his own efforts, he has bet on himself. Despite what I have just described, however, Rafe isn't really "gambling." He's simply applying his expertise in statistical odds calculations within atypical marketplaces—marketplaces he often *invents.*

Rafe is currently an adviser and an investor in BuggleMe, which connects celebrities to their fans through voice messages; iTripTV, whose goal is to "create a new and exciting way for people to interact with the world's travel destinations through cutting-edge mobile and digital media technology";[57] and a slew of other projects. His company Expert Insight has produced instructional DVDs with some of the most well-known names in their respective fields, ranging in topics from magic to pool to poker. He is an active angel investor who helps young companies get off the ground not only financially, but strategically and technically as well. In so doing, he creates the opportunity to "dabble" when it comes to the projects in which he invests his time.

Some of Furst's more recent projects include partnering with a fair trade coffee company positioned to help farmers in the Dominican Republic and a scalable, modular disaster-relief-shelter venture that is initially focused on providing assistance in Haiti but that has the potential to grow into something that is quite sustainable, as it is essentially "cheap housing that a lot of the world needs," according to Daniel Horowitz, one of Rafe's team members. Furst's philosophy in terms of what he is looking for when picking which ventures and entrepreneurs to work with? "Young people doing amazing things—we're just trying to support them." Rafe's role is that of an incubator, or as the name of one of his endeavors directly implies, he is someone who truly can "accelerate possibilities." While he is always playing the odds, a good hand can be as simple as smart people with innovative concepts.

57. http://www.itriptv.com.

That afternoon, as everyone is seated crossed-legged on the floor of an office inside his brightly colored, modernly furnished home, Rafe polls the group regularly as I listen in on, and at a couple of points even contribute to, the conference call being held. Furst only further demonstrates his insight as he asks questions and ....

ne has jumped from a videoconference about media production and outreach techniques, to a conversation about philanthropy and alternative fund-raising methods, to a discussion about nutrition and designing a mobile food truck.[58]

Despite the diverse areas in which Rafe is engaging, what stands out is that the skills he brings to each endeavor are of similar origin. It is also clearly noticeable that these are all things he truly *enjoys*. A casual observer might be unsure as to whether Rafe is working or simply pursuing a bunch of hobbies that he loves. "I'm trying to spend more time working on things that really interest me," Furst explains. "I am trying to take control of my intentions." And one of Rafe's biggest interests is clearly his work related to promoting cancer research.

In 2003, Furst and Phil Gordon were looking for a charity to become involved with. "We wanted to find an amazing initiative, partner up with them, and raise money and awareness around a great cause," he tells me. Furst and Gordon decided to take what, to many, would be the

58. Rafe's wife, Laura Rose, is in the process of launching a mobile organic smoothie company, called Belicious Smoothies, which will send trucks to different locations to sell organic drinks, promote healthy nutrition, and raise awareness about the obesity epidemic.

road trip of a lifetime—embarking on a whirlwind tour of practically every major sporting event in the United States in a decked-out "Monster RV." They called this excursion the "Ultimate Sports Adventure," and it included stops at the Super Bowl, the NBA Finals, the Indy 500, the Final Four, the Stanley Cup, the Kentucky Derby, the World Figure Skating Championships, and the WSOP, among many others. On that trip they came up with the idea for Bad Beat on Cancer, which encourages poker professionals and amateurs alike to donate 1 percent of their winnings to cancer research.[59] To date, this initiative has raised over three million dollars for "cancer prevention research, education, and nationwide community outreach."[60] "After the road trip we [Furst and Gordon] were asked to become board members of the Prevent Cancer Foundation and have been on the board ever since." Years later, this is still a large focus of Furst's energies.

"A few years into my tenure on the board, a fellow board member at Prevent Cancer asked me to come to a conference that consisted mostly of scientists and cancer researchers, and I just kept asking more and more questions," Rafe tells me. "I was asking them *very* basic questions. What is cancer? Is it curable? What do we need to do to make better progress?" These questions, although they seem simplistic, are exactly the kind of intentionally counterintuitive queries that arise when someone from outside of a discipline is introduced to the space, creating vectors that have the potential to lay the groundwork for innovation and changed perspective. In this particular case, the questions became the foundation for Furst's most recent project, "What Is Cancer?" which he envisions as having a multipronged approach, scope, and reach.

"That conference led to the idea of doing a documentary—we're trying to think of what's effective in terms of hammering home various

---

59. Supporters of the Bad Beat on Cancer include Phil Helmuth, Chris "Jesus" Ferguson, and Phil Ivey. If you don't know poker, these are three of the greatest players in the world.

60. http://www.preventcancer.org.

messages. Obviously there's the message of prevention, but I feel like there's a bigger message. How can we use science, 'Science 2.0' essentially (which is also the alternate name for this project), to advance the progress? I'm trying to work at communicating this vision through writing and visuals, online presentation, film

solution, is the end goal. "I'd like to create a bit of a video-shared social network for both researchers and the general public alike," he says, when asked about his broader concept for the project. "I am always looking for like-minded people who want to contribute in some way."

As Furst explains all of this, he walks me through an impressive multimedia presentation that includes a graph comparing the rapid decrease in heart-disease-related deaths since the 1950s compared to cancer-related deaths—which have basically remained stagnant. One image portrays geographic cancer clusters in America on a state-by-state basis adjusted for age and illustrated on a color-coded map depicting disease prevalence. While numerous environmental and genetic factors are known to be either causal or contributory in the onset of cancer, the degree to which cancer rates vary geographically is quite dramatic when visualized. Of course maps like these are readily available to doctors and research scientists, and have been intensely studied by experts at the Centers for Disease Control and Prevention, public health practitioners, and the National Institutes of Health for decades. What is of interest to me, however, is that Rafe Furst—the tech whiz, odds calculator, possibility accelerator, and world poker champion—is looking at data normally scrutinized only by epidemiologists. I found myself wondering what could happen if his multidisciplinary approach provided some

Renaissance-level insight à la Leonardo da Vinci or Alberti, and a significant contribution to the field of cancer research.

*For the rest of us, the key question is how to
combine our unique interests and skill sets to create
a microclimate for change and innovation of an
appropriate size and scale within our own lives.*

A month later Rafe invited me, along with a small group of other people, to participate in an online meeting to discuss financing and investment possibilities for a new venture called Vokle. Appropriately, the Vokle investment meeting actually used the Vokle platform, since it happens to be a cutting-edge method of hosting live interactive events online.[61] While I was watching and listening to Furst during the Vokle presentation, observing the analytical approach he brings to far-reaching and diverse topics, it became even clearer that it would be almost impossible *not* to define him as a modern-day polymath. By employing a multidisciplinary approach over the course of the last twenty years, Furst has been able to pursue multiple passions at once with enormous success. Instead of accomplishing the *work* of one person, he is living the *lives* of five or ten.

*Application of skills across disciplines can create diverse
work-life flow while fueling the type of innovative thought
often necessary to instigate Renaissance-level change.*

∽

LEAVING SANTA MONICA that day and driving back toward the Hollywood Hills, I wasn't thinking about vitamin D, the probability of winning at Roshambo, geographic cancer-distribution patterns, poker,

61. Al Gore used Vokle the following day for a worldwide educational "town meeting," which he cohosted with Sally Ride, the first female American astronaut to enter space, and Dean Kamen, the inventor of the Segue.

angel investing, Leonardo da Vinci's seemingly short attention span, or Alberti's stunning discovery of the obvious. Rather, what I was thinking about was that just like Rafe Furst, nearly all of the successful individuals I had been speaking with were employing a multidisciplinary approach in the execution of their

of Renaissance-like thinking. And this, in many cases, is best achieved by the implementation of a multidisciplinary approach. We have to understand that while rock smashes scissors, scissors cuts paper, and paper covers rock, the success algorithm itself is far more complicated—that a route to success may lie more in the application of the fresh perspective that is only possible when a mathematician looks at artistic technique, a systems expert looks at entrepreneurship and disease prevention, or perhaps when a musician sees an opportunity to green the environment, or a theologian finds a way to incubate start-up companies.

> *Employing a multidisciplinary approach can facilitate the cross-field pollination of ideas. This can provide a fundamental and proven way to infuse innovative thought into intellectually confined spaces, which, in turn, can yield unexpected opportunities that can be the foundation not only for the careers but also for the lives we are seeking.*

↜

BENJ GERSHMAN IS the bass player for the alternative rock band O.A.R. (Of A Revolution), a group he joined with three friends at age fourteen. More than fifteen years and piles of accolades later he invited me to a concert that the band was playing in Boston, where I interviewed him as we were walking through the Bank of America Pavilion, an outdoor concert venue that sits beautifully on the waterfront where the Charles River meets Boston Harbor.

The Pavilion is the city's top summer music venue, holds roughly five thousand people, and just about everyone will tell you there isn't a bad seat in the house. It's the middle of the afternoon and the weather is perfect, with a breeze coming in off the water. The amphitheater is empty save for the band—who are about to begin their sound check—their support staff, sound and light crews, and a few security guards. The last time I saw Benj we'd had a beer and watched World Cup highlights at a barbershop in downtown Manhattan, discussing everything from the band's efforts to provide assistance to war veterans to the pros and cons of mainstream media, and from pop culture's influence on career decisions to photography.

Today we are talking about greening businesses and the concept of being carbon neutral—specifically pertaining to the live music scene. Millions of pounds of recyclables are still thrown into conventional trash cans each year at concerts across the country despite efforts by some artists, promoters, and venues to increase recycling programs. The simple problem is, Benj tells me, for a lot of venues, "It just doesn't make financial sense yet. It comes down to the bottom line, and that's where artists can step in." In this regard, he is a passionate advocate for an initiative he has helped organize and coordinate with his bandmates called the "O.A.R. Green Dream," which began in the summer of 2008.

"On tour, year after year, playing to thousands and thousands of people, you begin to think about not only your personal effect but also the effect of the masses," Benj says. "The footprint was just so huge. I started to think, 'How do you do anything about this when the venues you play don't recycle? What do you do if the people in the crowd don't understand that it's important to recycle the plastic cups they use over the course of the night?' To me, watching people toss cups or cans on the ground from the stage was really frustrating. It got to me, and it built up and it built up, and when we were lucky enough to start playing shows that were ten thousand people plus, I started doing the math and realized how many pounds of plastic ~~~~

first tour that was entirely carbon neutral—we offset all of the emissions, and it's also a really positive element for the community of concert attendants, as our eco-village stamps our tours with a fun, interactive component that is also responsible and educational," he explains. "One of our next goals," Benj tells me, "will be to backtrack through our entire touring career and try to offset all of our previous emissions as well. So eventually O.A.R. will be completely carbon neutral, and also pass on, in a noncontroversial way, that experience to our fans."

Benj introduces me to a couple of the employees of the Green Dream, who are working to prepare a large tent with information about the cause in anticipation of that night's concert. He points out green receptacles spaced about every hundred feet or so around the venue, commenting that the Pavilion is a lot more green-friendly than many other venues of this size. "There can be a lot of red tape," he laments, "but fortunately some venues and promoters 'get it' and are really supportive and proactive."

Benj references a single tour from the previous summer (2009) that collected roughly eight thousand pounds of recyclables along the way through the band's efforts, emphasizing the key role that artists can play when it comes to initiatives such as this—ensuring that these goals are actually accomplished. We begin to discuss the concept of putting things in piles in order to understand their size and scope. How do you visualize eight thousand pounds of recyclable waste? That's four tons.

What does the average town produce in a day? A week? A month? How does one conceptualize a number like that? I tell Benj about the massive pile of plastic balls that Mickey McManus of MAYA Design discussed with me not long before—a visual aid to help comprehend an otherwise relatively intangible number. "What does four tons of glass, plastic, and aluminum actually look like?" I question. Benj, intrigued by this concept, makes a note to himself to look into the statistics before joining the band onstage for a sound check. At the concert that night the venue quickly became packed with over five thousand people, and I watched as every receptacle was filled, emptied, and refilled, and information was disbursed to interested parties at the Green Dream tent.

The next time I see Benj, it's a few months later and we are back in New York City. He is surrounded by a nearly impenetrable fortress of journalists, fans, friends, and critics at his debut photography exhibit at the Morrison Hotel Gallery, a prestigious space that hosts exhibits from the finest music photographers in the world. Tonight it's Benj's turn, and he is displaying his own photography. All of the pieces in the exhibit would go on to sell out.

"The first photo stuff I ever did was back in seventh grade, and then a few years later I worked at a camera store while in high school," he would later explain to me. "I also took some pictures when I went to Israel during my senior year of high school. I lived there for two months and studied history, and then my program would go to all of the locations where these historical moments happened. It wasn't specifically geared toward Judaism—we studied all religions and faiths, interacting with people from all walks of life and backgrounds. It was a truly amazing experience to have. I turned eighteen when I was there, and I was thinking of possibly joining the military when I got back to the States," he says. "But when I came back from Israel I realized what I wanted to do and how many freedoms I had as an American and how lucky I was, and I knew that music was going to be the vehicle to take me to the places I wanted to go in my personal life."

Benj decided to leave Ohio State after his sophomore year and "put college on hold to pursue a career with O.A.R.," he tells me. "The endeavor of college was to find a career, and circumventing that with something I loved, I felt no reason to hold off from pursuing it," he explains. "We made the decision that we had to go for it now—we thought if—

we were in our early twenties and on the main stage with Sheryl Crow and Train, which was unbelievable. Maroon 5 was playing the side stage. It was a fantastic experience, not just for the music but for learning the way the business works. It was very educational. We are all very involved in our business and wanted to know what was going on out there. It was the perfect opportunity for market research," he reflects. "There's no course to prepare you for what you have to learn to live on the road and stay healthy and run this kind of business and infrastructure— how to adapt your production and shows from venue to venue. We made so many mistakes, and it's great that we did, because now we are very efficient. It's always a challenge to be good at a business, and we had to figure it out as we went. It was *us* on the line—no one else. If the van broke and it was snowing, we had to push it up the hill."

With regard to photography, Benj says, "It wasn't until we started traveling consistently that I said, 'Okay, I want to do this'—this was around 2003. I enjoyed documenting what the band was up to and the places we were visiting. I would rent cars and just drive around and take pictures." Evoking thoughts of the humanist thinkers of the Renaissance, Benj tells me, "I liked capturing man's interaction with nature. I'd follow power lines rather than just wandering off into the desert. This enjoyment of our country is another aspect of where the Green Dream came from."

Benj didn't start out with the intention of becoming a professional photographer. For a long time he simply wanted to photograph for fun—"for my family and friends," he explains. "I wanted to understand the science of photography and develop my own style. I prefer to take one shot of something I wish to capture—I don't like to set up scenes or do multiple takes. Eventually I started to feel like a 'real' photographer— you could hand me any camera and I would understand what to do and how to do it. Playing a live song, for me, is very similar to capturing an image—it feels the same because you can't start over once you begin," he tells me. "It's an instinct more than it's a thought."

Benj's photography mentor, Paul Natkin, who has been shooting bands for decades, encouraged him to take his work to the Morrison Hotel Gallery. "The exhibit was over a year in the making, and I knew that it could 'legitimize me' as a photographer. But that's not why I did it," he explains. "It was because someone who I respected and who believed in me told me that 'this is the right thing to do.' I wasn't doing it for the 'career' aspect of it, but because a person I admired and looked up to told me this was the next step. I was so excited that my first exhibit was at Morrison Hotel and involved my closest friends and bandmates. Knowing that I had these other social roles that I work on, Morrison enabled me to get my foot through the door and now, as a next step in my photographic career, I aim to use these artistic images outside of my exhibition 'Rock, Cause (O.A.R)' to evoke change," he tells me. "It's great to know that I'm not the only one with these ideas—it reinforces for me that I'm doing something worthwhile. If you're an artist, some-times you ask yourself, 'Does anyone care about this as much as I do or as much as we do? Will someone find meaning in this?'"

Not long before, Benj and I were on the phone discussing the concept of life versus career and the importance of avoiding the mentality of being designated to one "box" when it comes to defining oneself. "I have so much time. I'm in no rush. I want to do it thoughtfully and properly,"

Benj told me, referring to *any* project he might undertake. "There are all these things I want to do, and I need to remain focused on keeping myself on the right track." (In regard to checking of boxes, it's more like checking off a lot of smaller boxes and grouping them into one big box.) He ultimately defines himself as an artist who utilizes a multidis...

I'm taking courses to get a degree in global business and public policy—I actually have a final exam in a couple of weeks. Business law can be overwhelming," he confesses. (He ended up getting an A in the course.) "Sometimes I bite off more than I can chew on purpose because I think you need to challenge yourself in this world, and as an artist I'm fortunate enough to be able to work on whatever I want. Having a relevant education—even if it's self-education—is just so important," he tells me. "I have a writing project; I have my photography; I recently gave a speech at the Apple store in SoHo, addressing being a touring musician and photographer in a difficult world climate; and the band is making great strides with our recycling program." O.A.R. is also preparing to release their seventh studio album following up their RIAA-certified platinum single, "Shattered," Benj tells me.

It used to be that when someone asked, "What do you do?" there was a simple answer. "I'm a cook." "I work on Wall Street." "I'm a doctor . . ." In this day and age, more and more individuals are involved in so many different projects and areas of interest that they have trouble answering that seemingly simple question. This isn't to say that there are no longer cooks or doctors—people who pick a single, vertical career path and stick with it. But there is another option.

*Become a member of a subset of the population that is
diversifying their own lives in order to accommodate as
many of their varying interests as possible, while at
the same time bringing a new and multidimensional
perspective to each new endeavor.*

These are the polymaths, the people who have trouble answering the question, "What do you do?" "Well . . ." For many, the more appropriate question might be, "What are you doing *right now*?"

The next time I see Benj, we are in Los Angeles as he and his bandmates take the stage for a sold-out concert at the House of Blues, just as they did in Boston a few months earlier for back-to-back nights at the Bank of America Pavilion, and as they have so many times before over the course of the last fifteen years. This is a group that has been together for half of Benj's life, sold out Madison Square Garden, played some of the biggest festivals in the world, and sold well over one million records—but despite all of these accomplishments, his horizontal interests cannot be contained by vertical barriers. Benj and O.A.R.'s members are as, if not more, inclined to want to talk about a 2007 USO tour—during which they entertained and met thousands of military personnel in Kuwait and Iraq—than they are about any concert or album sales. The Green Dream is arguably his biggest philanthropic passion, though Benj and his bandmates are involved with several other social causes, including the education initiative Heard the World[62] and Paralyzed Veterans of America.[63] All the while, Benj is pursuing other creative outlets that include his photography, writing, and activism, and, of course, music.

"I have directed my life very specifically. I go through these phases of creativity. Music has provided this for me," Benj acknowledges. "I

62. http://heardtheworld.org.
63. http://www.pva.org.

will have two months free where I can focus on something between tours. All those things are about being very directive in regard to the time that I have, and how I choose to spend it is very deliberate."

Like Rafe Furst, Benj cannot be defined in monomath terms. Backstage at the House of Blues after the concert, it isn't your typically

OBJECTIVELY SPEAKING, IT is clear that it is easier to be a polymath if one is able to function with financial independence on the level of Rafe Furst, Benj Gershman, or one of the patroned artists from Leonardo da Vinci's time. And while many of the people I had been speaking with found the funding for their successive ventures in the coffers of their early success, there are individuals from all walks of life who take a multidisciplinary career approach and pursue a variety of endeavors with little or no preexisting financial support. Simply understanding that we don't necessarily have to pick a single career or work in only one field—that we are never boxed in by education choices or early career decisions, and that we all have mobility—can lead to multidisciplinary success.

Instead, we can simultaneously, or sequentially,
pursue a number of different interests.

⌒

IT'S 7:00 P.M. on a Thursday night in San Francisco, and downtown is bustling. I'm texting back and forth with Mike Del Ponte, making sure that I'm standing in front of the right restaurant. Mike's first feature in

Fast Company had run just a week earlier, which forced me to reformulate several questions I had already prepared for him. I'm also curious to meet his friend, Zane Wilemon—a twenty-eight-year-old priest who runs a forward-thinking nonprofit called CTC International[64]—who was a late but welcome addition to our dinner plans. Zane spends six months out of every year living in Kenya, delivering medicine, clean water, and basic education to children.

As we ordered Indian food and collectively realized that we were all headed to the same event later that night, only further lightening the already relaxed atmosphere, we began to speak about Mike's rapidly emerging venture, Sparkseed, which he hoped to use as a vehicle to propel the building of what he envisioned as the "Silicon Valley for social entrepreneurship." Mike's background and unique way of thinking help to define him as a person who is on an interesting and noble mission.

Mike received a graduate degree from Yale Divinity School in 2008. He initially enrolled with the intention of becoming a priest or a teacher but decided to make a change. Realizing that he could potentially accomplish more in terms of helping others, giving back, and pursuing a multitude of interests by spreading a message through the power of social entrepreneurship—that he could reach more people while still maintaining his core values—Mike decided to change directions and start a nonprofit he called Sparkseed. Sparkseed would serve as a platform to enable young, college-aged social entrepreneurs and start-ups by providing essential resources, expert consulting, a support network, and financial backing as a means to help viable social ventures and nonprofits become established and grow. Even Sparkseed's press releases and application guidelines emphasized, "This is not simply a grant; this is a social innovator development program. While we do provide seed funding to our social innovators, you should not apply for this reason. The training, tools, and connections that we offer are the real value-adds."[65]

64. Comfort the Children.
65. http://www.sparkseed.org.

"We've been partnering with like-minded companies and organizations while also helping to facilitate connections," he told me that night. One manner in which Mike facilitates connections on a larger, more personal scale is through hosting a weekend networking conference called, entirely appropriately, "Dangerously Ambitious." Il-

⌐⌐⌐⌐⌐⌐

⌐⌐⌐⌐⌐⌐

tionships were made. When you are actually involved in group activities with people, as opposed to just sitting and listening to a keynote speech, you are able to learn far more and create bonds through the interactions." This was an opportunity for Mike to extend his reach, this time as an event organizer and promoter—connecting people and ideas.

Since Sparkseed was providing capital, be it financial (up to eleven thousand dollars per company), business or philanthropic resources, advice, social media, Web consulting, or otherwise, Mike and his team have had the somewhat unique privilege of being involved with multiple endeavors simultaneously under one umbrella. One of the ventures that Sparkseed partnered with is EcoScraps, founded by Daniel Blake while at Brigham Young University. EcoScraps takes food waste from commercial chains and "turns it into a one hundred percent organic soil amendment."[66] This is food waste that would otherwise be occupying a landfill were it not diverted; but by converting the food waste, EcoScraps has been able to sell top-quality soil amendments based on raw materials—the food waste— that are free for them. EcoScraps not only has the ability to reduce landfill space but also to reduce carbon emissions by "up to twenty percent."[67] In

66. http://www.sparkseed.org.
67. http://www.sparkseed.org.

backing this venture, Sparkseed helped enable EcoScraps to grow both faster and more efficiently, while simultaneously allowing Mike and his team to work on a project in which they have extreme interest.

Another one of Sparkseed's backings is INeedAPencil.com, founded by Jason Shah in 2007 while he was still in high school. The mission is to provide free SAT preparation to students who can't afford private, expensive test-prep classes. Since its inception, the venture has gone on to help over thirty thousand students and counting, raising participants' cumulative test scores by an average of over two hundred points. With Sparkseed's assistance, Shah has been able to advance his cause with more efficiency and speed. He has been featured on CNN and in *People* magazine as a "Hero Among Us," and in 2011 he was running the program from Harvard, where he was a student.

For Del Ponte, the ability to work with companies this diverse has been appealing on many levels. Being able to support and advise one socially minded enterprise that is helping divert food waste in a sustainable fashion, while providing resources for another young social entrepreneur who is helping to leverage equality in education through free test preparation, as well as aiding and supporting dozens of socially conscious endeavors Sparkseed has backed is, as he puts it, "quite a gift."

Of course these are only two examples of myriad socially responsible start-ups that Sparkseed has backed, and while there is a wide range in terms of *what* each does, there are at least two traits that they all have in common. First, they were the ideas and concepts of students who are focused on the field of social change, however defined, and second, they were part of Del Ponte's vision of a rapidly growing "Silicon Valley for social entrepreneurship." Through Sparkseed, Mike created a platform for young entrepreneurs to learn, grow, network, collaborate, and share resources and ideas. He has gotten to explore and to learn about a multitude of new concepts and forward-thinking ideas on a daily basis. One minute he could be on a conference call discussing an initiative that focuses on youth who want to increase the quality of the food available in their schools, and the next he could be advising a company that is developing intelligent software to assist in outsourcing "complex business tasks without sacrificing quality."[68] Yet again, Mike is someone who has applied a multidisciplinary approach in his own life. He cannot be defined by checking off one box, simply because h... f

after backing and supporting multiple successful enterprises, winning awards, being showcased in national media, and during the same month that INeedAPencil was featured in *People*.

"We've hit the milestones we wanted to reach, and we've helped a lot of great businesses. The possibility of replicating this model, essentially incubating social change ventures, now exists," Mike said optimistically. He told me that Sparkseed would continue to remain active in the sense of supporting their current partners, but they will not be taking on new projects. He wants to reach people in a different manner, and on an even larger scale. "I want to affect five hundred million people, not five hundred thousand," he said.

As far as closing the doors on Sparkseed and looking to the future? "I'm psyched," Mike says. And I believe him, despite my surprise at the news—he was shutting down a rising entity that was garnering national attention *by choice*. "What does it mean to 'go out of business'?" he asks me. "Is it a sign of failure, or is it a sign of moving on to something bigger and better?" A few weeks later, Sparkseed was featured in a *Wall Street Journal* article as an example of a successful company that was incubating socially conscious start-ups. As I read it, knowing that Sparkseed

68. http://www.sparkseed.org.

was shutting down, I was left wondering whether this venture was akin to one of Leonardo da Vinci's unfinished projects—a brilliant piece of work set aside for others to learn from as Del Ponte moves on to pursue even larger endeavors, or if this is simply one of those remarkably successful smaller accomplishments that litter the landscape of a renaissance.

We don't have to be defined by a single interest, one career, or conventional thought. Often, the most rewarding results may be found when we apply the polymath approach in our own lives.

8

■

If one advances confidently in the direction of
one's dreams, and endeavors to live the life which
one has imagined, one will meet with a success
unexpected in common hours.

—HENRY DAVID THOREAU

S ETTING OUT TO write this book, one of my early observations was based on the simple premise that success is often
the result of an extraordinary response, or series of responses,
to relatively ordinary life events. During the course of this process, I
came across a few people whose success stories fell outside of this original premise in the sense that their achievements didn't stem from ordinary life events at all. Instead, theirs were stories of success that originated
from rather *extraordinary* occurrences. Although an extraordinary
response to each of these circumstances was still required, the success
itself resulted from uncommon events. In an effort to understand how

these stories fit this model, I proceeded to search for commonalities—looking at not only what they had in common with each other but also at any similarities they had with the other success stories that I had been researching, most of which had sprung from seemingly more ordinary life events.

What emerged is that the binding thread of all these stories of success, regardless of whether they originated from an ordinary or an extraordinary event, is passion.

In fact, a salient factor and critical keystone in the construction of success, however it may be defined, is *unwavering* passion. None of the high achievers I encountered was merely "doing a job." None of them reported that they set out "just to earn a paycheck." They weren't keeping a seat warm, performing their duties in a perfunctory manner, punching a time clock, leaving early out of ambivalence, or pursuing their careers solely as a means to survive and pay the rent. None of them were cogs in the slave 'n' save system or lukewarm about their career choices, and not a *single* one of these successful people said that the goal when starting out was to "get rich." Success, wherever found, is always rooted in genuine passion. In fact, all of the individuals I encountered have personal, unrelenting, sometimes irrational, unmitigated, "eat, drink, and breathe it" passion for what they are doing. As a result, the commitment they have to their careers is both resolute and sincere.

This particular form of passion is ultimately a critical factor in what can ignite and then sustain success. It fuels everything from the drive and motivation that constitutes the necessary work ethic to the creative, innovative, idea-building mind-set that is a prerequisite for a high degree of accomplishment. And this passion also manifests in another notable manner. People with this type of passion wake up in the morning and find that there is no clear definition as to what is "work" and what is "personal." They are able to craft a life-work milieu in which they can pursue areas of personal interest as a means to financial stability *and* life satisfaction, one in which the only difference they notice between Wednesday and Saturday is in the name of the day. Their "work" is actually a combination of things that they love

It follows then, that if we are looking to forge our own route to success, we must first identify something about which we are genuinely passionate. The underlying and paramount importance of "finding what we were born to do" is supported not only by the simple, age-old adage to "do what you love" but also by the stories of virtually everyone I spoke with—from Bobby Chang and Ellen Gustafson to Ido Leffler and Adam Braun, and from Elizabeth McKee Gore to Shawn Fanning, just to cite a few examples. Digging a bit further in a quest to unearth what is, on the surface, a very simple concept, it became clear that some people know from a very young age what it is that they were "born to do," whereas others have to work quite a bit harder to find out exactly what that is. And knowing what you were born to do could not be better exemplified than by the story of Jamail Larkins.

⤻

JAMAIL LARKINS WENT to space camp when he was in the fifth grade. It might not be your "typical" summer camp, but it was something he wanted to try. "I loved the experience. I was chosen to be the 'shuttle commander' on our little mission," he tells me, laughing. That experience led him to develop an even deeper interest in flight, and when he got home he purchased Microsoft Flight Simulator and began to learn the basics of small aircraft operations. "I used it on a daily basis," Jamail says. "I was hooked."

Wanting to explore this newfound love of flight even further, at the age of twelve Jamail decided to write to a Delta Air Lines captain, telling the captain about his desire to become a commercial airline pilot. From him, Jamail learned about the Young Eagles Program, which offers kids between the ages of eight and seventeen the ability to go on general aviation flights. He got access to a database of pilots involved with the program and decided to start making some moves. "I randomly selected a pilot nearby based on an address that I recognized. So I called him." At first, the pilot was a bit confused and taken aback, asking Jamail, "How did you get my number?" But that didn't last for long. "He would later go on to tell me that I was the first kid ever to call him, and he respected me for that," Jamail says.

Soon, Jamail was signed up for his first flight. "We went to the local airport," which was near his home in Augusta, Georgia, he tells me, "and I remember flying over my middle school and my house and saying, 'Wow, this is what I want to do. This is who I am going to be.' The pilot even let me fly the plane a little bit," Jamail enthuses.

From there, Jamail began taking regular flight lessons, quickly mastering the controls and honing his skills inside the cockpit until he had the qualifications that would have made him eligible to be licensed by the FAA. There was only one problem. He was thirteen years old—three years shy of the required age minimum. "How can I stretch my dollars?" Jamail began to ask himself. "I was a middle-class kid, and I realized that flight lessons were getting really expensive. I got to a point where I could handle the plane," he explains. There was no longer any need, at least skillwise, for a flight instructor to accompany Jamail on his flights. But federal regulations mandated that he be supervised. "I was basically paying someone to babysit me," he says. So, Jamail decided to petition the FAA to allow him to obtain his license three years early.

"Here I am, a naive thirteen-year-old kid, not realizing how difficult it is to get an exemption around a federal law." So he decided to get creative. "Maybe if I go to another country to get my license, then come back, the FAA will have to acknowledge me," Jamail reasoned. "I wrote letters to about one hundred companies and organizations, hoping to

imagined.

"It gave me a chance to become the national spokesman for the Young Eagles Program, which was an amazing honor," Jamail says. From there, another interest began to emerge, partly due to his need to finance his flying time. "I became friends with John and Martha King, who allowed me to become a distributor for the King School.[69] It still wasn't paying what I had hoped, but I was doing pretty well for a sixteen-year-old." Instead of working at a coffee shop or the mall like most high schoolers, Jamail was selling GPS equipment to pilots. This led him to develop a love of business and sales and provided a significant personal reward as well. "I was able to purchase my own airplane during my senior year of high school," he tells me, casually.

As a result of the press surrounding his Young Eagles position and his growing reputation as one of the brightest young pilots in the country, when he was fourteen Jamail began to develop a relationship with the director of admissions at Embry-Riddle Aeronautical University. Jamail called him every other Friday for years—not exactly "normal" behavior for a young teenager. His passion for business, however, eventually led

---

69. The King School is an aviation-supply distributor.

Jamail to consider attending Wake Forest University instead, thinking that a business degree might be "more useful" than one in aeronautics. Friends and family were advising Jamail, "Don't go to Embry-Riddle. Go to a business school."

Jamail was leaning toward taking their advice and applying to Wake Forest, but the admissions department at Embry-Riddle found out through a magazine interview that he was considering other options. Engaging in behavior typically reserved for top athletic recruits, the admissions director flew to Atlanta to convince Jamail to visit the campus. And he agreed. Jamail tells me that he spent a total of ten minutes at Embry-Riddle before making up his mind. "It's weird. I've never been to a school where an airplane flies overhead and everyone looks to see what type of plane it is." Needless to say, he didn't apply anywhere else. While attending Embry-Riddle, Jamail continued to shine, performing professional aerobatics in air shows—and he was one of the youngest in the United States to do so. "I still do it, but not as much anymore. Primarily because it takes a lot of time to stay sharp and efficient with that sort of flying," he tells me.

During that first flight when he was twelve, Jamail thought he wanted to be a commercial airline pilot. But now he was more interested in business and smaller aircraft, and he wanted to find a way to combine his interests under one umbrella. In order to accomplish this, he got his start in commercial aircraft sales in 2006.

"I loved the concept of buying and selling planes. I loved transactions of that size and how complicated they are," he explains to me. In 2008, Jamail launched Ascension Aircraft, which was a derivative of an earlier company, Larkins Enterprises, that he started at age fifteen. "The concept behind Ascension is that aviation is a mature, older industry. We wanted to be a little more useful and have a fun vibe. Customer service was the most important aspect," he tells me. And because of Jamail's passion for flight and his business acumen, Ascension quickly

became a force to be reckoned with in a highly specialized and seg-
mented market.

"I hope to see Ascension become the premier private aviation firm
in the industry. There is no 'top dog' in this particular niche," Jamail
explains. "Most people know airlines, like Delta or American, that

inant market share," Jamail tells me. Ascension focuses on general aviation, brokering deals for small planes to mid-sized jets. As far as a
full-service experience, maintaining, and facilitating aircraft for their
clients, Jamail aspires to be recognized as the top firm in his field. "We
want to be the go-to company."

In 2009 Jamail Larkins was named the number one entrepreneur in
America on *Inc.* magazine's annual Top 30 Under 30 list, with Ascension Aircraft and Larkins Enterprises combining for a projected revenue of $8.4 million.[70] At the time, Jamail was twenty-five years old and
had only four employees. He has also been recognized as one of the
country's top young entrepreneurs by CNBC, *BusinessWeek,* and *Black
Enterprise*, and Congress awarded Jamail with a Certificate of Special
Recognition for his work in the field of aviation. In 2011 Jamail was
named a Young Global Leader by the World Economic Forum.

Jamail is quick to acknowledge what a critical role passion has
played in his success thus far, noting that his love of aircraft and flying
is something that potential clients can find contagious. "It's been a great
experience. We are selling planes to universities, individuals, and private

70. http://www.inc.com/30under30/2009/profile_ascension_aircraft.html.

companies. I can combine all of my passions. If I want to fly a particular airplane, I just put my name on the list," he tells me enthusiastically. "We have airplanes all over the country, including California, Mississippi, Georgia, and Oklahoma. We either manage the planes or lease them out." In regard to combining business with flying, he says, "I love the chase of the next deal. It's fun now." Jamail has clearly crafted a life for himself in which passion is the driving force—and he found this passion before he was even a teenager.

"It has been an amazing experience to be considered, at least in some people's eyes, as a leader in this space," Jamail tells me. "Every day is different. We are adding clients and winning accounts that make me really excited. When I look back, thinking that I would be an airline pilot, I honestly had no idea that any of this would be possible," he admits candidly. "I'm so glad I kept an open mind. Don't be blinded by internal goals. I would have missed out on all of these amazing opportunities."

❧

JAMAIL IDENTIFIED HIS passion at an unusually young age, he pursued it relentlessly, and he kept an open mind. As a result, he was able to craft astounding personalized success. But in the two examples that follow, both stories of success rooted in extraordinary circumstance, it is clear that for some people, what they were born to do, that resolute passion that is a prerequisite to success, simply and unequivocally finds *them*.

These examples are of particular interest because rather than being extraordinary stories of passion-driven success rooted in favorable conditions fostered by fortuitous opportunity, they are success stories that emerged from extraordinary misfortune and suffering. This, in and of itself, is of paramount importance because it serves as a demonstrative marker that success can be cultivated even in the *worst* of circumstances.

And this points to the fact that within the vocabulary and the culture of success there is a subtle, yet significant, attitudinal and perceptual nuance.

To individuals pre-wired for success, the possibility of defeat is never actually defeating.

nosed with chondrosarcoma, an extremely rare form of cancer that affects only about a thousand people each year. He underwent treatment, got a clean bill of health from his doctors, and fueled by the knowledge that he beat the disease, resumed his life where he had left off. Although he didn't know it, his battle wasn't over yet. Within a brief period of time Doug would go on to be diagnosed with, undergo treatment for, and overcome two additional bouts with cancer—this time with malignant melanoma.

Not to be defeated, Doug returned to Brown University, helped the soccer team win three Ivy League championships, and started his own foundation—the Ulman Cancer Fund for Young Adults—geared toward "developing more dialogue" with young people about cancer. "I ran it out of my dorm room," Ulman explains to me, "and my goal in the beginning was simply to raise awareness about the impact of cancer on young adults and provide support." Before he graduated from college, Ulman's foundation was growing, he was—knowingly or unknowingly— laying the groundwork for a career in philanthropy, and he was already a three-time cancer survivor.

On October 30, 1997, Doug got an e-mail from then twenty-six-year-old cyclist Lance Armstrong, who had undergone treatment for stage-three testicular cancer and "had started the Lance Armstrong Foundation and wanted to check in, since we had some common experiences," Doug tells me. "We e-mailed back and forth for two years, and we shared many of the same goals when it came to awareness, prevention, detection, and research," he says. After a few years of idea building, their friendship and mutual respect grew, and in 2001 Ulman joined forces with Armstrong as Director of Survivorship of LIVESTRONG, the international cancer awareness and fund-raising foundation that is perhaps most recognized by the symbolic yellow wristbands that are sported by tens of millions of people across the globe. The objective of LIVESTRONG is to work "to identify the issues faced by cancer survivors in order to comprehensively improve quality of life for members of the global cancer community."[71] By the time that Doug joined LIVESTRONG, Armstrong had overcome his own battle with cancer and had already begun to establish what would be his record streak of seven consecutive Tour de France victories.[72]

In 2002 Doug appeared on fifteen million boxes of Wheaties as an "Everyday Hero" in recognition of his work in raising awareness and hope in the cancer detection and fund-raising space. Although his passion and life's work originated from his own life-threatening disease, he was able to harness this extraordinary misfortune and turn it into a passion-driven success, not only for himself, but for millions of people around the world as well. "Far more important than just raising money," Ulman tells me, "is the ability to empower a community."

In 2007 Doug was named CEO and president of LIVESTRONG. He sits on the Google Health Advisory Board and the executive board of the Ulman Cancer Fund for Young Adults. He is a member of the American Society of Clinical Oncology, was chairman of the National

71. http://www.livestrong.org.
72. In October 2012 Lance Armstrong was stripped of all seven Tour de France titles by the International Cycling Union and banned from competition for life because of doping charges by the U.S. Anti-Doping Agency. Armstrong later admitted to doping, and he resigned from the board of directors and stepped down as chairman of LIVESTRONG. The organization also officially changed its name from the Lance Armstrong Foundation to the LIVESTRONG Foundation.

Cancer Institute Director's Consumer Liaison Group for five years, and cofounded the LIVESTRONG Young Adult Alliance. When I asked Doug about working in the LIVESTRONG community, he said, "The best environment to work in is one that is naive and audacious. We are naive and audacious enough to think we can change the world but

strong, and the commitment of their employees, partners, and volunteers, LIVESTRONG has become a *tower*—with Armstrong a global ambassador more recognizable than most political figures. His athletic accomplishments allowed him to achieve even larger victories outside of the world of sports by providing a platform for LIVESTRONG to get its message out. The cause built an audience of hundreds of millions of people worldwide, with Armstrong becoming one of the most well-known athletes in the world, winning "Athlete of the Year" honors from the Associated Press a record four years in a row, from 2002 to 2005. "Because of the brand and Lance's visibility, we have the ability to mobilize and advance," Doug acknowledges proudly.

This cumulative media exposure has enabled LIVESTRONG to foster and facilitate change that is as broad reaching as it is personal, as idealistic as it is practical. While there are now representative and awareness-raising wristbands for causes ranging from clean water to heart disease to breast cancer, the yellow LIVESTRONG wristband is a universally recognizable symbol and was the first standout charitable "fashion accessory" of the last decade. (Its color is a reflection of the yellow winner's jersey in the Tour de France.) To date, over seventy million LIVESTRONG wristbands have been sold, and Ulman tells me that they expect to sell "in the neighborhood of seven million wristbands in 2010." Astoundingly, the wristbands have become so popular that street vendors in New York City sell illegal knockoffs of what is supposed to be a wholly charitable product.

One momentous and far-reaching consequence of LIVESTRONG's success, Ulman tells me, aside from the obvious immediate benefit of raising funds to build a support network for cancer awareness, prevention, detection, and support from the sale of the LIVESTRONG wristbands, is that the organization has provided a model for other philanthropic groups to pattern by implementing similar, parallel techniques to promote their own causes. "If you told me fourteen years ago that I would be wearing something like a bracelet that enabled me and so many other people to express ourselves, I wouldn't have believed you," Doug says, acknowledging exactly how influential the foundation has been in terms of raising awareness and creating dialogue. "Wars like this are won with hand-to-hand combat, not in labs."

"The wristbands are far more important than the money in the sense that we are bringing together, engaging, and empowering a community of people who wear their support on their wrist for others to see," Doug says. "In terms of public awareness, the benefits are wonderful. Getting young people involved and educated is the most empowering aspect." When we spoke, Doug had just returned to Austin, Texas, from a trip through China and Norway, where he was raising awareness on behalf of the foundation, meeting with partners, and delivering presentations along the way.

"The biggest gains over the last ten to twenty years have been in early detection, which is the reason survival rates are up. Cancer is being caught and identified earlier and earlier. But the real progress," he tells me, "will be made if more money is directed toward finding the causes of the disease—not solely sustaining the lives of those already affected." In regard to finding a cure, Doug tells me, "When people think of curing cancer, a lot of them think of it as one 'disease,' but cancer is obviously an umbrella term we use to classify hundreds of diseases." In terms of finding cures, like so many other visionary leaders from different fields I had been speaking with, Ulman emphasizes the emerging role of the private sector. "The lines are blurring. The days of nonprofits solving these issues alone are over."

What LIVESTRONG has accomplished and helped create far surpasses any statistical data that can be captured in an annual report or financial analysis. There are too many intangibles—numerous variables that have had an unquantifiable effect. Rather than functioning solely as a self-promoting entity, because of the staggeringly large numb... f...

the passion of Lance Armstrong and Doug Ulman—two young men battling and overcoming potentially fatal diseases, men whose seemingly catastrophic circumstances were not viewed by *them* to be defeating. Instead, they took those unwanted and unfavorable circumstances and leveraged them in such a way that, along with a core team of like-minded, committed individuals, they built a beacon for change. As a result, they have helped prevent countless deaths through their campaign to create awareness and promote early cancer detection, while helping those already diagnosed and/or affected by providing community support on a variety of levels.

Although this life mission was pulled from extraordinary circumstances, in refusing even to entertain the possibility of defeat, they both approached their misfortune with a passion and mind-set that cultivated immeasurable success.

Objectively speaking, very few people in the world operate on the level of Doug Ulman or Lance Armstrong—and most people or organizations don't have access to the type of media exposure and branding available to LIVESTRONG. This said, endeavors stemming from extraordinary circumstances, when coupled with unwavering passion, don't necessarily require such high-profile exposure to succeed. Further, though very few of us will face a personal battle of the same magnitude as Ulman and Armstrong at such a young age, there are endless extraordinary events that can lead to passion-driven success if sourced from the pools of circumstance in which most of us see only defeat.

⌒

WHEN I WAS offered a pair of VIP tickets to see Bob Dylan at the Fox Theater in Oakland, California, in August of 2010, I immediately called Sean Carasso, founder of Falling Whistles, to see if he wanted to attend the performance with me. While Dylan represents for many the 1960s version of youth protest and sociopolitical expression, Sean's story is emblematically representative of this new generation's role in that same arena.

When Dylan came of age, the Vietnam War was raging, the civil rights movement was on the verge of exploding, and if you were under twenty-one and a citizen of the United States, although you still didn't have the right to vote, you could be drafted against your will to serve in the armed forces. Lacking the speed and interconnectivity of today's technology, the primary means of sociopolitical expression for young people involved the constitutional right to assemble. Physical congregation in the form of either violent demonstrations or peaceful sit-ins were the prevalent form of protest, and whether you participated in these protests or not, if you were young in the sixties you were a member of what would become known as the most outspoken, turbulent, and powerful youth generation in history. Without much of an outlet for expression or a viable platform for change, Bob Dylan, along with his now legendary peers from that era, voiced his opinions through music and poetry, using with revolutionary effectiveness passion-driven protest lyrics as a vehicle for social and political activism.

Fifty years later, Sean Carasso is a member of a generation whose music has, by and large, lost its sociopolitical message. Given that this new generation has access to outlets for voicing expression and propelling social change outside the arena of music, this is solely an artistic casualty and is not indicative of a change in generational motivation or intent. An obvious yet pivotal example of how much political power this new generation holds lies in the 2008 election of President Barack Obama. An unprecedented turnout among voters under the age of thirty-five is credited to a large online movement and grassroots campaign

⟿

WHILE SEAN CARASSO'S nonprofit foundation, Falling Whistles, can't compare in size or scope to LIVESTRONG, his story is representative of an entire subgroup of this generation who have taken experiences of world travel and recast them as significant pathways for personal growth, channeling passion as a means to develop life and career opportunities, new business concepts, and venues for meaningful social impact. In 2007, at age twenty-five, Sean quit his job as a personal assistant to John Paul DeJoria (the founder of Paul Mitchell and Patrón tequila) and embarked on a backpacking trip through Africa, in which, he says, "The goal was to get lost." After three months his travels brought him to the Democratic Republic of the Congo (DRC), where he found himself on the frontlines of a brutal civil war. "It's the deadliest war in our world," Sean tells me, "and no one is talking about it."

There are more rapes each year in the DRC than in any country in the world, and since 1996 it is estimated that this war has claimed the lives of over 6.9 million people.[73] As with every war, it is complicated by numerous tangential issues, but at its core is an economic war for

---

73. Nicholas D. Kristof, "The World Capital of Killing," *New York Times*, February 6, 2010.

minerals—specifically tin, tungsten, tantalum, and gold[74]—which are used in the manufacturing of electronic devices we use every day, including cell phones, computers, and televisions. These are "conflict minerals" that are extracted from mines controlled by rebel warlords. The miners themselves are often enslaved women and children who are treated brutally, and the profits generated from the mining of these natural resources are used by the rebel groups to fund the ongoing conflict. In a profoundly sad humanitarian and economic turn of events, the wealth of natural resources in the DRC is funding mass destruction and war instead of growth and prosperity for the nation.

During his first week in the DRC, Sean came across a military encampment in which former child soldiers were being held captive and beaten for committing "war crimes." Sean encountered five imprisoned boys (all under the age of fifteen at the time) who had escaped their captors and "ran to the national army for refuge." Instead of receiving help, the boys were being treated as war criminals. They were frightened, filthy, starving, and forced to stand all day and night in a makeshift prison cell. Their names were Busco, Bahati, Serungendo, Claude, and Sadiki. Sean tells me that before they arrived at the military camp, each boy had been "abducted by rebel soldiers, forced to kill, and forced to force others to kill."

When the boys were originally abducted they had been tortured, confined in a hole in the ground for twenty hours a day, and then pulled out for four hours of "training" so they could be indoctrinated as soldiers for their rebel captors. The boys too small to carry a gun were being sent to the front lines armed with only a whistle. Their purpose, Sean bluntly puts it, was twofold. "They were sent out at night to blow the whistles and scare away the enemy. Failing that, they were told to

74. Section 1502 of The Dodd-Frank Wall Street Reform and Consumer Protection Act, which calls for transparency and a reduction in use of these conflict minerals mined in the DRC, was signed into law by President Obama on July 21, 2010.

receive the bullets with their bodies and, in falling, create a blockade for other soldiers to hide behind."

What Sean saw left him understandably horrified. But rather than accepting these circumstances as defeating or beyond his control, he did all that he could with the little that he had. First he bought the child

Sean's experience and encounter with this humanitarian crisis ultimately became a full-time commitment to helping children who are victims of this war. He wrote an impassioned journal entry called "Falling Whistles" that he e-mailed to approximately eighty people, mainly friends and family, expressing his outrage and heartbreak over the conditions he was witnessing. The recipients, in turn, forwarded his e-mail to hundreds of additional people. Friends, and friends of friends, immediately began to respond asking, "How can I help?" "What can we do?"

When he returned to the States, Sean was broke and distraught over the ongoing conflict in the DRC. So much so that when his friends threw parties to welcome him home, not knowing what else to do, he would "yell erratically" that "people are dying." Even though he wasn't personally a victim, he responded as if he were. "One night," Sean tells me, "one of my best friends, Marcus Price, came to me with an old vintage whistle he bought on eBay. He put it around my neck and said, 'No matter where you go, keep those boys alive in your heart.'" Everywhere he went, people would ask Sean, "What's the whistle?" What followed was "an explosion of youth energy," in which Sean inspired others to work toward peace in the DRC.

Based on this passion, Sean founded the nonprofit organization Falling Whistles. He decided to "brand" the whistle to honor the children who were carrying them on the front lines—an image of war, death, and despair in the DRC could become a symbol of unity, peace, and solidarity back home. He sells the whistles bearing the organization's logo and asks each purchaser to become a "whistleblower for peace" by making "their weapon your voice." In purchasing and wearing a Falling Whistle, we can become advocates for victims of the war in the DRC. The whistle, Sean reasoned, since it is an unconventional fashion item, would attract questions. And those questions would lead to conversation. Conversation leads to education, and education leads to change. If people are curious enough to ask, they will be interested enough to listen.

To date, Falling Whistles has generated over three hundred thousand dollars in funding and provides both financial and resource support for the rehabilitation of over four hundred women and children "coming out of the war region." The whistles are carried in close to one hundred stores, including Curve and Atrium in New York and Fred Segal in Los Angeles, and have been worn by numerous celebrities including Beyoncé, Jon Stewart, Jessica Biel, Rihanna, and Gwyneth Paltrow.

While the ultimate goal is to end the conflict in the DRC, Sean and the Falling Whistles team are not deterred or defeated by the enormous complexity of this brutal humanitarian crisis. They are driven by pure passion. The passion that propels them toward each small victory along the way is fueled by the knowledge that with every whistle they sell, another person will become a foot soldier in *their* movement, and perhaps one less child may fall victim to the violence in the region. This passion found Sean in the form of the extraordinary—a military camp in the DRC in 2008—and now he is helping others find this same passion.

The extraordinary circumstances of someone
else's extraordinary pain became his own.

Sean Carasso may be armed with both the right to vote and the immense power and interconnectivity proffered by technology, but Falling Whistles' message to "Make their weapon your voice" is a throwback, in the best sense of the word, to the sixties and its generation of antiwar activists. Just like the musicians who picked up their instru

Shortly after my evening with Sean in Oakland, and after our follow-up meeting the next day in San Francisco, he would be off again, this time on a three-and-a-half-month tour of the United States in an RV with the Falling Whistles team, promoting their message and "building a countrywide coalition for peace in the Congo." They stopped in thirty-five cities to bring attention to the cause by screening a documentary film and giving a presentation of the Falling Whistles story, which is full of understandably powerful emotion and personal outrage. Sean, who supports himself on a modest budget that redefines minimalist for the average American, has described to me over the years several periods since the launch of Falling Whistles in which he "lost a good deal of weight" because he was giving every dollar he had toward saving the recovering children as he fought to get the message out.

"Dylan once said 'What's money? A man is a success if he gets up in the morning and goes to bed at night and in between does what he wants to do,'" Sean told me that night. Sean has unwavering passion for what he does. He wakes up every morning with grand goals and expectations. He doesn't entertain even the possibility of defeat. "I live out my liberty everyday, and anything less is unacceptable to me. Millions of men and women have died so I can be free."

Passion-driven responses to extraordinary situations can empower us to effect tangible change.

&

CONTRASTING THE SIXTIES and Bob Dylan against this current generation and organizations like LIVESTRONG and Falling Whistles, observing the role that drive and passion play in the construction of success, raises questions as to the position each youth generation occupies in the overall culture—from how young people are integrated into society, to how they voice and impart their opinions, to how they ultimately define themselves. Entrenched in the stories of these successful young people, I began to think about members of this current generation as a group remarkably similar, in many regards, to foreigners arriving from a distant land and needing to integrate into the existing economic and political landscape.

In the broadest sense, as a collective population, each generation reaches adulthood with its own unique set of social and cultural underpinnings. Influenced by the overall climate in which they were raised, each generation has its own vocabulary, its own perspective and motivations, its own command of technology, and its own particular spin on art, lifestyle, and politics, as well as the current world and business environment. This cyclical influx of "foreigners" collectively represents groups who must be assimilated into the broad sociopolitical climate of adulthood, as well as the business and economic environment, on an ongoing basis. While this initially manifests as a challenge to the existing institutional framework, it eventually becomes the foundation for fundamental and inevitable change. Rather than constituting an enigma, this is an influx that is, for all intents and purposes, part of a recurring economic and cultural migration—one which reappears in roughly twenty-year cycles—and the push factor is simply maturation.

Perhaps unknowingly and inadvertently, over the last few decades there has been a shift in the distribution of power, and it is incrementally skewing decidedly younger. As society relinquishes more and more power to the youth generation, sometimes intentionally through legislation (such as lowering the voting age to eighteen) and sometimes unintentionally (as in the unlimited access to rapid information feeds

.... previously exist if we display the same passion and commitment as Jamail Larkins, Doug Ulman, and Sean Carasso.

When an interconnected generation with a unique tool set,
escalating power and influence, and a global worldview
brings unwavering passion and commitment to the table,
while simultaneously recognizing opportunities for success
where others see only defeat, the stage is set for a paradigm
shift of paramount and unprecedented importance.

9

HARNESSING CAPITALISM FOR GOOD

*Why Companies That Generate Direct Philanthropic
Dividends Will Be the Trademark of This Generation*

■

It is said that the present is pregnant with the
future.

—VOLTAIRE

N MY QUEST to deconstruct success by analyzing the individual
stories of high achievers, I was searching for resonating commonalities. As much as I was carefully listening to what people
wanted to talk about *individually*, I was even more interested in learning what they wanted to talk about *collectively*. It was these patterns and
repeated themes that became the foundation for the tenets presented in
each chapter.

As the interviews progressed, I began to notice that one of the most
compelling and consistent messages that came out of these conversations didn't concern how the successful people I was speaking with got

to where they are *now*. Rather, it was what they were telling me about where they are heading *next*. And even though I interviewed them individually, collectively the majority of them were telling me the same thing.

...., just like housing starts and factory orders do for the overall economy—then this would mean that, more than likely, the rest of us are heading to that same place too. And the reason that this is so important is self-evident.

> *If this is where the economy is heading, then*
> *this is where the jobs will be as well.*

Before examining exactly where that is, and in order to frame just how significant this shift might be, it's worth revisiting Copiapó, Chile, and the men who were trapped for sixty-nine days in that collapsed copper mine two thousand feet beneath the ground. As you might suspect, during this time they were, for the most part, living in the dark. And this particular fact played out in a very interesting way.

When the miners emerged from the escape capsule, roughly one every forty minutes over the course of a full day, it was broadcast live in a wall of media coverage. What aired on television screens and computer monitors—with an estimated one billion people watching around the globe—was a life or death real-time drama of unprecedented magnitude. And when they stepped to safety, each and every one of those miners was wearing a pair of Oakley sunglasses.

When the rescue mission was being planned, doctors raised serious concerns over possible damage occurring to the miners' eyes when, and if, they finally arrived aboveground and stepped into the daylight (or into the artificial light used by the rescue team at night) after such an extended period of time in the dark. In response, Oakley, the American eyewear company[75] known for sports performance gear and high-end style, shipped thirty-five pairs of ultra-dark wraparound Radar sunglasses to the rescue team in Chile as a means of protecting the miners' eyes. The doctors were so concerned about ocular damage and possible vision loss due to increased retinal sensitivity that they sent the glasses down into the mine, told the men to put them on prior to entering the escape capsule, and instructed the miners not to remove the sunglasses under any circumstances once they reached the surface.

If the glasses had been purchased at a store like Sunglass Hut, they would have retailed for over $6,000 (roughly $180 apiece), and of course it cost far less than that to manufacture them. When Oakley became aware of the potential problem, they donated the sunglasses to the men. As the miners stepped out of the escape capsule, a few of them removed their helmets as they stood before the cameras and embraced their families—but they all followed those doctors' orders. Not a single miner took his Oakleys off. When all was said and done, the media exposure that Oakley received as a result of this event was estimated by Front Row Analytics to be worth in the vicinity of forty-one million dollars.[76]

Despite the gigantic dollar figure assigned to the underlying value of this impromptu media exposure, no one suggested that Oakley had anything on their minds other than helping and saving the miners. Oakley certainly didn't create or seek out this opportunity—it just happened to innocently fall into their, undoubtedly grateful, corporate lap.

75. Oakley was founded in California in 1975 and merged with the Italian company Luxottica Group in 2007.
76. http://www.cnbc.com/id/39650306.

Of equal and interesting note, it was also widely reported that in the days prior to the miners' rescue—well before they put on those sunglasses and climbed into the escape capsule, and well before they even knew if they would survive—all thirty-three of the miners signed a pact to band together and sell their story as a group. And the price tag

.... poised to potentially make money, Oakley got free advertising, and media outlets and their advertisers profited from this disaster as well. Even when faced with life-or-death catastrophic situations, capitalism is at work—front and center. We create and exploit microeconomies. We do it on Main Street, we do it on Wall Street, and we even do it when men are trapped in a copper mine in Chile.

Whether an equity, a commodity, a derivative, or a life-or-death human drama, there is an underlying value that is constantly being assessed for profit potential. And virtually nothing is off-limits.

〜

PROGRAMS ADDRESSING GLOBAL need and humanitarian issues are rooted, either directly or indirectly, in capitalism as well. Up until recently, most of these initiatives have been structured around a donation-driven economic model funded either through government programs (themselves funded through money collected via taxation) or through donations collected from the private sector. But in order to pay the taxes that support government programs—or to make a donation to help fund a private-sector initiative—an individual or corporation must first generate income through a capitalistic endeavor.

The problem with this donation-based system lies in three fundamental and inherent flaws. The first of these revolves around the fact that donations are typically collected at the very end of an economic cycle—after all other expenses have been taken care of. Second is that the need-based capital generated through this system has been universally recognized as inadequate—the amount of global need grows disproportionately faster than dollars can be collected, despite all good intentions. The third flaw with a philanthropic and charitable giving model dependent on tax-based government funding or private donations—which includes everything from children collecting pennies for UNICEF while trick-or-treating to corporations and private foundations donating millions and even billions of dollars to need-based initiatives and humanitarian causes—is that, as Jessica Jackley referenced when discussing the value of microloans, the vast majority of donation-driven transactions are financially and emotionally terminal. The interaction abruptly ends when the cash changes hands, and it often leaves both the donor and the recipient diminished in the process. Basically, donor-driven programs aren't sustainable,[77] they don't engage people on an emotional level, and to generate funding they simply rely on end-of-the economic-cycle donations—successive tax rolls, a new batch of "trick-or-treaters," and the lure of next year's corporate write-off.

But for the last few years, there has been a significant shift and a rapidly growing trend among entrepreneurs to launch for-profit companies that market products and services that create sustainable revenue streams to support charitable causes, often by aligning a specific product with a specific need, while emotionally engaging the consumer in an ongoing

---

77. Of course there are exceptions, including initiatives like the Bill & Melinda Gates Foundation (with an endowment of over $36 billion) and companies like Newman's Own (the food product line set up in 1982 by actor Paul Newman that donates 100 percent of after-tax profit and has generated over $300 million for charity), which are, at least financially, self-perpetuating.

manner. In so doing, these entrepreneurs and their companies are addressing all three of the flaws in the existing donation-dependent system.

First, these new initiatives aren't reliant on tax dollars or soliciting donations after all other discretionary spending is complete. Rather, they utilize a "substitution model" to generate funding for humanita-

g .... day-to-day purchases.

Clear examples of this model are both TOMS and FEED Projects—they are selling products that we would buy anyway. People buy shoes and people buy bags, so why not buy shoes and bags that provide footwear and nutrient-fortified meals for children who desperately need them? Especially if the quality and the price is the same or better than that of competing brands. We, as consumers, are simply being provided the choice of using our dollars slightly differently by buying one product instead of another. We get a product we need or want and in so doing receive a feel-good social dividend—both at the point-of-purchase and with the continued use of that product or service. We have the opportunity to make a public statement about ourselves by making the initial purchase, while also aligning ourselves with a cause as the use of the product serves as both a private, and often public, affirmation of our own belief systems. And, most important, we are provided a way to use our consumer dollars and our everyday purchases to effect real,

78. Paul Newman's company was established at the end of an economic cycle in the sense that he didn't start Newman's Own until he had become one of the most celebrated and respected actors of the century and had a name he could leverage. His reputation allowed him to set up his product line as a nonprofit. The Gates Foundation is endowed with funds donated at the end of an economic cycle as well—in this case toward the end of personal earning cycles.

quantifiable change. There are some potentially groundbreaking financial and psychological dynamics at work in this model.

As Blake Mycoskie referenced earlier, this generation wants to "be a part of movements and surround ourselves with like-minded people that share our view of the world." And many of these new initiatives are providing a way for each of us to do this on an everyday basis. These social entrepreneurs are simply operating within a niche of the philanthrocapitalism space, redirecting both consumer dollars and business expenditures in a manner that yields humanitarian dividends at no additional net cost to anyone. In so doing, they are effectively creating a microeconomy based on generating profit in order to aid philanthropic initiatives. It is a marketplace that is relatively new, expanding exponentially, and redefining capitalism—for good. It's almost impossible to see any downside to "profit with purpose," creating a sustainable stream of capital for a cause, and offering a quality "purchase with benefits" to the consumer. Everyone wins.

In fact, the upside is so enormous that companies like these are in a position to completely change the landscape of business and philanthropy.

These businesses are not built around an unclear, difficult to discern, "sometime in the future, some small portion of our revenue or profits will go somewhere to do something" model. Rather, they establish a clearly delineated, very direct connection between a specific product or service and an easy-to-understand, quantifiable "give" with every transaction. And this isn't a bunch of "feel-goodery" that only works in theory or on paper, nor does it represent an after-the-fact tag-on to a marketing strategy. The two companies cited in this example—TOMS and FEED Projects—have not only been on a mission to address humanitarian issues since their inception, but they are also worth millions of dollars. They provide a give that is both transparent and direct, they employ people, and they turn a profit.

By structuring companies as for-profits and building giving into the business models, the structure sustains the give and encourages even more entrepreneurs, who see the coupling of profit and giving as an appealing and creative alternative, to enter the space. As a result, the mass consumer base and the broad business community are invited to

business owners and conscious consumers can
have their capitalistic cake and eat it too.

〜

MOVING FORWARD IN the evolution of business, and in particular in the evolution of the for-profit business of philanthropy and need, there is going to be a parallel evolution occurring with regard to the *ethics* in this space. As we delve further into the arena, many people will rightfully become a bit less comfortable with the concept of "profit with purpose" if it begins to edge closer to "profit on pain." And this is an important, yet oftentimes difficult distinction to make.

Over the course of the last several years there has been an increasing dialogue as to the ethics regarding the right to profit from need, yet it is hardly a new debate. The battle over the distribution of HIV/AIDS drugs in Africa and whether or not pharmaceutical companies—who spend billions on R&D—are entitled to profit from the sale of these life-saving drugs is a clear example of this ethical dilemma. What it boils down to are the uncomfortable questions of who should profit, by how much, and when is *any profit at all* ethically unsavory?

Yet another demonstrative example of this debate, the blurring of the lines between humanitarian efforts and for-profit enterprises and the recent trend toward solving specific issues by monetizing those issues for corporate profit, is the complex and ongoing legal fight and ethical concern over the patent rights for Plumpy'nut—the peanut paste that is credited by almost everyone as a "miracle cure" for severe acute malnutrition. It is inexpensive, ready to eat, tastes good, and doesn't require clean water or rehydration in order to be consumed. And it works. The French manufacturer of Plumpy'nut, Nutriset, owns the patent rights to this ready-to-use therapeutic food (RUTF) and is fighting an international, multiparty legal battle to have the patent rights protected. Nutriset generated sixty-six million dollars in 2009, with the bulk of that revenue coming from the sale of Plumpy'nut.[79] Those challenging the patent range from companies that want to be able to profit by selling the paste themselves to individuals and organizations who feel that *no one* should profit from a global health issue of this magnitude—especially when the solution is as simple as a peanut paste with added sugar and vitamins.[80]

Since the fundamental core of these issues essentially rests on who gets to live and who gets to profit from the solution, this debate becomes enormously complicated. But regardless of where we stand on these ethical questions, as more businesses move toward social entrepreneurship and monetizing philanthropic endeavors, they will be simultaneously profiting from, and serving, humanitarian need. And when the ethical issues are removed, the equation is simple.

private pain + profit with purpose =
corporate gain + less private pain

It is so simple, in fact, that many established companies are running to attach themselves to humanitarian issues as if armed with a

79. http://www.nytimes.com/2010/09/05/magazine/05Plumpy-t.html?pagewanted=4.
80. UNICEF purchases over 90 percent of its supply of Plumpy'nut from Nutriset's factory in France, and then distributes it.

pair of handcuffs shaped like dollar signs. Philanthropy, causes, and need have become primary marketing and branding tools, and whether or not this ultimately works to serve the greater good will simply come down to how many of these companies have integrity.

One distinct mainstream marker that underscores this shift in con-

million dollars each week toward classroom funding.[81] And the trend has been viral. Home Depot, ExxonMobil, McDonald's and Lowe's, to name a few, all advertise their philanthropic endeavors—oftentimes more so than their products.

What many companies are selling, or in some cases *trying* to sell, is that social dividend. They are attempting to improve brand image by linking their product line with social responsibility. For some companies the donation to charity is part of a genuine desire to give back to the community. For others it is a line item in their budget—no different from manufacturing costs, shipping expenses, or the price of producing a commercial. But unlike social entrepreneurial ventures like TOMS, FEED Projects, and thousands of other companies like them that were designed from day one to provide a humanitarian dividend, for many of the companies making the "conversion," these dividends are an "add-on" and often, first and foremost, more of a financial decision than an overriding corporate philosophy. The hope is that these social dividends will pay off from the standpoint of brand image and, ultimately, lead to increased profit.

---

81. Target has been donating 5 percent of its income to community causes for over 50 years. I'm not criticizing them for advertising this fact.

A question arises as to whether the corporate give is deemed to be a loss leader—something that businesses are willing to lose money on just to get more consumers through the door—or if it is a genuine reflection of corporate ethos. But perhaps the more important question is whether the motivation behind *any* donation or social dividend *really* matters at all.

If the world's corporations are generating sustainable funding for humanitarian causes and can raise awareness and effect change for these causes while simultaneously turning a profit, and if new start-ups originate with socially conscious agendas woven into their DNA, they all have the potential to become giant turbines for generating good. As a result, all of us—whether on the consumer side, the entrepreneurial side, or as employees of these companies—will have the opportunity to participate in this cultural and economic shift.

Because this is where we are heading.

⌒

WHICH BRINGS US back to the young, successful, leading "economic indicators"—the barometers of the future. When discussing where they are heading next, the majority of the individuals I spoke with indicated that they are venturing into the complex global arena of philanthro-capitalism and corporate social entrepreneurship, not through traditional philanthropic channels, but by building for-profit companies that will address a wide variety of humanitarian issues. And regardless of how anyone ultimately feels about this shift, it is very clear that we are all about to become social currency traders.

Our economic future is based on a goods-and-services-substitution model in which traditional everyday purchases yield philanthropic and humanitarian dividends.

This concept sits right with a generation of young adults who, as a result of technology, feel more connected than ever to the issues that face the world community. In fact, many people from all generations are looking for more than "just a paycheck" when it comes to their careers, and they are now being provided with the option of leveraging

ing new. In the 1930s during the Great Depression, flour was sold in printed cloth sacks that women used to make quilts. They *needed* the flour, but they *wanted* the fabric. So they bought the brand with the nicest patterns. As we move forward and the dividend, the added benefit that comes with a product, is serving a humanitarian need, funding education, providing clean water, medical aid, and the like, we will begin to see the groundwork for what will essentially become the "Philanthropy Wars." As more players enter the space, competing to offer the best social dividend along with their products or services, there will be good players and bad players—and there is the potential that consumers will get lost in all the "noise."[82]

Obviously there are many underlying ethical concerns as we try to identify a universal code of accepted practices as this marketplace continues to evolve in a way that may actually permit the dollars generated to catch up to, and match, the need. The same need that is progressing exponentially faster than traditional philanthropic and charitable models

82. In April 2011, for example, *60 Minutes* ran a story calling into question the ethics and actions of Greg Mortensen, the best-selling author of *Three Cups of Tea*, and his organization, the Central Asia Institute, which had reportedly been misusing funds that were meant to be used to build schools in Pakistan and Afghanistan.

can possibly address. There is no question that there is a tremendous amount relying on the integrity of good winning out. And one example of good winning out lies in Causecast, an enterprise that is engaging people by pushing philanthropy and cause-based programs into the mainstream.

∽

BRIAN SIRGUTZ IS the president of Causecast, a for-profit company with a philanthropic arm that manages and promotes nonprofit initiatives. "Our goal is to be the gateway for content and actions on the Internet for anything cause related," Brian tells me. "In a sense, we're kind of the middle men. We monetize this through our technology and through advertising revenue sharing." Causecast provides and distributes exclusive, socially conscious content that is accessed by millions through their various partnerships (the *Huffington Post*, MTV, and AARP to name a few) and promotes initiatives that include the Download to Donate program, which works with musical artists ranging from Dave Matthews to Shakira and from Linkin Park to She and Him.

"We have four hundred unique, exclusive tracks by different artists," Brian tells me as we navigate L.A. traffic on a Friday night in late August. "Once you make a donation, you get a code. When you bring that code to the Download to Donate website, not only do you get a track or an album from that artist, but you get a subscription for a year." That subscription gives each donor access to exclusive content that is only available through the Download to Donate platform. The funds from the purchase are then given to Music for Relief, which in turn funds various programs that are helping to rebuild Haiti—a great value-add to music fans and a great social dividend at the same time.

One of the interesting aspects of Causecast's role in this space is that, unlike some of the other companies already mentioned, they offer services, content, and platforms as opposed to more traditional consumer goods. Essentially, Causecast is helping to provide exclusive content that is used to fund worthy causes by creating a "shelf," or in this case a platform, to showcase them on—as well as the technology to deliver that content and engage the consumer. In 2010 Causecast worked on a project with Ben Stiller called "StillerStrong," which utilized a viral video campaign that included appearances by President Clinton.

... ... provide news content for a section called IMPACT. The relationship was structured in such a way that Causecast would provide the content while splitting the advertising and sponsorship revenue generated by the section. IMPACT showcases stories about important humanitarian and social issues, offering readers news stories with the added benefit of being able to participate in the solutions.

"We launched the IMPACT section with a story of a family that needed help. The mother couldn't afford medication that would keep her from going blind, while at the same time she had just enough to afford her daughter's medication for the same disease. So the mother chose to go blind so that her daughter could continue to see," Brian tells me. The response to the article was overwhelming. "In thirty-six hours we raised upward of thirty thousand dollars through the *Huffington Post* community, and Arianna Huffington is on *Larry King Live* talking about the power of story, context, and giving back. And all of a sudden here is this idea that became a viable platform to help people," he says. "You can actually have curated actions from the content being delivered because there is context and story around it."

As Brian eloquently states when asked about their overall mission, "The idea isn't to bring people to a cause, but to bring the cause to where they *already* are." And he goes on to discuss just how powerful this model can be.

"The impact has been this amazingly quantifiable data—we have helped reach millions and millions of people who have read our content and, as a result, have helped raise millions and millions of dollars," Brian says. "Then there are the intangibles. For example, I recently got an e-mail from a guy who essentially said, 'Thank you for putting my blog post on the front page of the *Huffington Post*—when you put it up there all these Peace Corps alumni got upset that the government hadn't released thirty-five million dollars in additional funding for the Peace Corps.' This set off a chain reaction of people writing to their representatives and then putting pressure on the executive branch to release those monies. And eventually the money was released," he tells me.

As far as the future of cause-based marketing, Brian is optimistic that people will become increasingly engaged with the world around them through companies like Causecast and forums like IMPACT. "The launching of the IMPACT section has been amazing. We have some of the most influential contributors, from Bill Gates to George Lucas to Ashton Kutcher to George Clooney to President Clinton and Secretary of State Clinton, and everyone is chiming in with regard to issues that are important to them," he tells me enthusiastically. "They aren't separated from society or the world."

Echoing the sentiments of many of the visionary leaders I had been speaking with, Brian doesn't necessarily view the traditional vertical models of capitalism and philanthropy as mutually exclusive. "Statistics are showing that all businesses that incorporate philanthropy into their DNA have seen an increase in employee retention and stronger consumer loyalty. By allowing customers' purchasing power to support causes via buying a product and allowing their employees to take more active parts in their community, giving back is better for the bottom line in retaining employees," he tells me.

"Everyone should have the ability to take some sort of action if they want to," Brian says. "It shouldn't be an arduous process. But that's exactly what it still is at this point, so that's what we're all about. Social media only works so much. You need to have the context or story to drive it, especially if you don't have the face-to-face encounter. Movements are not created or built just on people connecting with a 'general'

from the ground up—and in many cases with limited resources—are able to bring the same business sense, mind-set, and honed skills from the for-profit space and apply them to social and humanitarian issues, we open the doors for a broad-based, multidisciplinary approach to problem solving. By injecting a completely fresh perspective, they are setting the stage for a possible set of entirely new solutions. And by "allowing" them to run these initiatives on a for-profit basis, we are not only inviting many more talented people to participate in generating these solutions, but we are also allowing them to do so with the most powerful economic tool we have: capitalism.

⌒

BOBBY CHANG, WHO used design principals to deconstruct a way to teach his daughter how to ride a bike, to lower his golf score, and to build the company that became the most recognizable supplier of Apple cases in the world, has left the day-to-day operations at Incase to

83. Brian Sirgutz became the senior vice president of social impact, responsible for all cause-related content, for AOL/Huffington Post Media Group following the 2011 merger.

dedicate his time to philanthropic initiatives. Bobby has been engaged with philanthropic endeavors in the past, but his most recent initiative, H.E.A.L. Together, is certainly his most ambitious.

H.E.A.L. is an acronym for Helping Expand Awareness for Life and is a for-profit organization with a philanthropic arm that is meant to serve as both a platform to raise funds and create a community for the world's philanthropic initiatives—be they spawned from for-profit companies, conventional charitable organizations, or any other like-minded group, for that matter—to network, cross-pollinate, and share information in a communal and transparent space. And like Cause-cast, H.E.A.L. Together is designed around yet another innovative model that harnesses day-to-day consumerism to effect and curate social change.

"In the late nineties, when we started Incase, we were in the dot-com era," Bobby tells me. "Back then it seemed like anyone with a tech start-up and an e-mail address was getting a large check to start or sell a company. But now, we are in the philanthropic era. H.E.A.L. is the next stage of my philanthropy and design work, and the goal is to push humanitarian problems and disease into the social space. This is where we can generate truly creative problem solving," he explains. Bobby follows this statement by asking me a question.

"Did you know that measles is still a huge problem?" I didn't know this, but I feel a bit better after Bobby tells me that he didn't either until someone told him about it. "I assumed that measles was along the lines of smallpox or one of those 'old' diseases that was long gone—completely eradicated. Learning about issues like this and then addressing them is what we are seeking to accomplish," he says.

Chang goes on to describe one of H.E.A.L. Together's first big projects, a partnership with the Red Cross that links unique, traceable serial numbers to bandages that any business or organization can buy to support a cause and then distribute to customers or supporters. Each bandage represents a corresponding donation that can be tracked any-where in the world using GPS technology. The "bandages" are literally bandages, and they serve as an advertising tool for the issuing entity, while simultaneously engaging the emotional involvement of the recip-ients, as the attached serial number allows them to track the corre-

be quite possibly the best example of a positive work environment I have ever encountered),[84] the implications of the initiative and the tech-nology they are using became even more apparent.

"If you received the serial number for this bandage from your bank or local store," Christian demonstrates to me with staggering ease, pointing as the GPS pin begins to drop into location on the computer monitor, in this case indicating that the bandage has been traced to a town in Haiti, "you can literally have that engaging experience of becoming involved with a cause or a movement because you can actu-ally see where the impact is being made. The more tangible it is, the more people become involved and invest their time and mental energy, the more that will be accomplished." Once again consumers are en-gaged through a personal connection—this time via GPS. It costs them nothing, since the give, which was paid for by the hypothetical bank or corresponding brand, has been embedded into their day-to-day

---

84. The H.E.A.L. Together headquarters is essentially a house and yard—complete with a living room, kitchen, shingled garage, synthetic lawn, tree house, and a sliding-panel bookcase that reveals a "secret" screening room—constructed within a historic Los Angeles art gallery. The goal being not only to create a work environ-ment that people don't want to leave, but one they want to invite their friends to as well. In a sense, going to "work" is like being "home."

activities—providing a feel-good dividend from something as ordinary as a trip to the bank.

"We started to joke that it would be the first bandage in history designed to *spread* a virus rather than contain it. We also chose the bandage for the obvious symbolic meaning," Christian says. "Also, virtually everyone has worn a bandage at some point in their life, so there's no need to explain it, and the consumer acceptance is already there. You can stick it on your skin, your shirt, your jacket, your backpack, your laptop, the back of your phone, your car bumper, your helmet, your surfboard, or anywhere you might put a sticker," he explains.

"We hope to reinvent the structure of charitable giving," Bobby tells me. "We want to allow people the opportunity to not only give more but give more often." And he is not simply referring to the old-school, one-prong approach of donations when he says "give." These initiatives are aimed at creating substantial and sustainable relationships of support. These are all equally, if not more, valuable forms of currency because they engage the larger community in problem solving on an ongoing rather than a transactional basis.

"People respond to what they experience," Christian reinforces, pulling up one slide after another on his iPad, each presenting a different problem, conceptualized solution, and plan of action, "not what they are told. We think outside the box. How do you engage people on a different level?" he asks, followed by an even more intriguing question.

"What if we gave an entire city cancer?" Caught slightly off guard, I take a moment to think about what this even means. Christian goes on to explain a hypothetical concept meant to both engage people and form "communities within communities," fundamentally capitalizing on a form of crowdsourcing problems, in which ownership of an issue is assigned to a larger community. In this case, Christian discusses an entire city, or even several cities, using their collective force—whether that be financial, intellectual, creative, or otherwise—to solve a problem.

"What if we gave an entire city cancer?" he repeats. "Not the people, but the actual city. Then we let the people go in search of the cancer in order to save their city. This would allow people to learn early detection and the types of cancer they should be looking for, not only in the city but in themselves," Christian explains. "We plan to make it an interac-

the community as a whole and assigning it a problem to solve. This collective engagement has the potential to achieve massively productive social change, if this type of consumer-driven community involvement becomes the norm. So much so, in fact, that H.E.A.L. has both coined and trademarked terms like *Funanthropy*.

HealLA launched in late 2010 as a "microsite" focused on the community of Los Angeles, with the overriding concept of connecting capitalism and need in a very specific and direct way. Functioning a bit like Groupon, whereby they create strategic and mutually beneficial connections between a specific give and a defined "get," HealLA establishes relationships and sets up deals with local businesses that yield social dividends. When consumers go to the HealLA website they can make a donation to one of the featured charitable initiatives, and then H.E.A.L. Together gives a corresponding deal to the consumer "as a reward for the good deed."[85]

If, for example, you wanted to book a hotel room for a business trip or a vacation, you can donate twenty-five dollars to a cause on the HealLA website, which in turn will grant you access to a reduced-rate hotel room through one of their partners. In effect, the substitution

85. http://www.healla.com.

model allows the twenty-five dollars off your room expense to be donated, for example, to a mission in Los Angeles that will provide a bed and a shower for one night for someone who is homeless. It costs the consumers nothing more than they would have paid for the hotel room in the first place, generates a feel-good benefit through the realignment of purchasing dollars, and, obviously most important, provides a bed and shower to the recipient of the give. It costs the companies or organizations that make the donations nothing more either—they have simply repositioned their advertising dollars in the form of a give. They associate themselves with a good cause and simultaneously gain a new way to get customers "through the door"—where they may spend even more money on goods or services. Everyone wins.

Once again, this social dividend is attained with
no net increase in dollars spent by anyone.

⌁

THESE ARE ONLY a few examples among thousands of great consumer-driven, for-profit philanthrocapitalistic enterprises that are facilitating change by harnessing capitalism in new and unique ways. And they are accomplishing this in a manner that costs the consumer nothing—in fact, many consumers are getting a value-add. These companies are engaging people as a community and altering our expectations with regard to the purchasing power of our dollars, effectively inviting us to become conscious consumers and to change the manner in which we address humanitarian need. It is very likely that the route to solving many pervasive global issues may not lie with the "experts" and the traditional channels, but instead with a combination of our newfound interconnectivity and the power of the crowd to both financially and intellectually crowd*source,* crowd*fund,* crowd*ideate,* crowd*execute,* and crowd*solve* pervasive problems that have been "unsolvable" to date.

We may be the generation that will be credited with retooling capitalism by linking day-to-day consumerism with global philanthropic and humanitarian issues as we extract the enormous strength of each individual micropurchase to create a collective, macro impact. The reason for this shift is that the mechanism of change itself has evolved, in large part due

a cycle of negativity in which the integrity of any individual cause is diminished because there are too many insincere players in the space. If this happens, then the collective impact could be the reduction of the integrity of the entire marketplace. But like all great instruments of potentially immense power, in the right hands, profit with purpose, social entrepreneurship, and philanthrocapitalism have the ability to dramatically alter the economic model used to address poverty and need. It is becoming very big business and has the potential to instigate very big change.

It is in many of these new initiatives that we see the collision of everything discussed in the previous chapters—finding the right company to work for, approaching problems from unconventional angles, sourcing the crowd, becoming a disruptive force, taking a multidisciplinary approach, and pursuing passion. Simply through our consumerism and job choices, we can be part of this movement. In fact, whether seeking employment or starting our own businesses, giving and profit with purpose are, or will become, core components of the companies we work for or the businesses we own—much like the Experience MBA emerged as an addendum to a poor economy and a changed generation. And for the overall world community, this is exceptionally good news.

*The personal and global ramifications of these collective
initiatives will become almost immeasurable, affecting
not only some of the world's largest humanitarian
problems but redefining capitalism and, in turn,
the job market and the overall economy as well.*

10

Never confuse a single defeat with a final defeat.

—F. SCOTT FITZGERALD

W HEN I BEGAN to consider whom to interview for the final chapter of this book, my primary objective was to identify a story that would best represent, in an encapsulating and comprehensive manner, all of the component tenets culled from the individual stories of success I had been writing about over the course of the past year. I knew that I needed to identify someone who had responded to ordinary events in extraordinary ways, had a different view on traditional education, had taken on risk, built a business with an integral focus on company culture, attacked problems by approaching them from unique angles, built and sourced a powerful network, operated as a disruptive force, and channeled passion. Basically, I was looking for a polymath who had run the table while cultivating something quite a bit larger than formulaic, run-of-the-mill "twentieth-century" success.

Further directing my thought process was the fact that when I sat down to write this final chapter, I had been observing, in a very acute manner, the intersection of life and work. I was propelled in this direction by the understanding that no one I had been speaking with had achieved the type of success likely to be left at the office at the close of the business day or that was confined in any manner by the conventional barriers associated with the terms *job* or *career*.

The type of success that I had been both observing and documenting for the better part of the past year doesn't reside at a corporate address or take place during normal business hours. Rather, it is embedded so deeply, aligned so seamlessly with each individual's self-identity that it operates within its own time zone and is carried home at the end of each day. Success of this nature, undoubtedly and precisely because it is such a perfect fit, so personally crafted, so hard fought, and so passion-driven, is, in just about every instance, played more like an extreme sport than a nine-to-five job—manifesting more as "who I am," than "what I do."

For most, this type of life-defining success
is the stuff of waking dreams.

Since the majority of the companies and organizations showcased in this book are philanthrocapitalistic—enterprises rooted either in social entrepreneurship or defined by profit with purpose—I decided that I wanted to interview someone for this final chapter who is running a for-profit business and is involved with a company that is selling a traditional product in what is, in essence, a conventionally "unsexy" space. The argument was that in order to conduct a "drop test" for the success tenets outlined here, they had to be applicable in the strictly for-profit sector as well—and I didn't want to profile just any successful for-profit business. I was looking for a company that had reached the summit of a seemingly insurmountable peak. I wanted to speak to the CEO of a billion-dollar corporation.

Knowing that I needed to start this drop test from a very high place,

I also recognized that there was one critical aspect to achieving success, however defined, that I had yet to touch upon, despite having discussed the topic with every single person I interviewed and spent time with. I wanted to find someone who could address this final tenet in a nontra-

~~~~~~~~~~~~~~~~~~~~~~~~~~~~~counterintuitive manner.

life is that they all have, what I perceive to be, both an unusual and healthy relationship with failure.

As much as success might define them,
failure auspiciously doesn't.

Of course, any and every successful person will tell you that they have failed. That, in fact, they have failed many times. The difference, I noticed, between these high achievers and the rest of us, is that even though we all may reflexively regurgitate the same clichés about failing and the value of lessons learned ("If at first you don't succeed, . . . "), successful people actually believe them in a substantially deeper manner. I consistently observed that those in the top tier of success don't *internalize* failure in the same way that most people do. For them, failure is not a reflection of self. It is completely objectified and isolated, believed to be an experience from which to learn, a measure of the inability to accomplish one specific task at a single moment in time, or the result of variables that likely have little to do with the individual in question. Nothing more.

Successful people perceive failure as normal. Just an ordinary mid-week nothing. More of a hiccup than a death sentence. Failure is not a definitive blow or insurmountable obstacle but rather an interesting anomaly. Failure is neither an embarrassment to be swept under the rug nor a gauntlet being thrown down. To successful people, failure is a bit interesting—perhaps an intriguing conundrum or an oddity worthy of observation.

As a result, for successful individuals, failure is a means to refinement and redirection that actually leads to exponentially more potent success.

During the hundreds of hours I spent with cutting-edge ideators, entrepreneurs, and leaders, regardless of their respective goals or definition of success, failure was never a topic about which they were guarded or reserved. In fact, in many cases successful individuals were even *more* enthused to discuss their failures than their successes. And for this reason, when I asked people about failure, I consistently got some of the best stories and often the most interesting, engaging responses. For them failure isn't a destination, but rather one of the small towns they happened to spend the night in while en route to the big city.

An unemotional relationship with failure is a contributing factor to why people succeed.

Fear of failing simply isn't an obstacle. Rather, each failure provides direction and creates clarity as they move one step closer toward achieving their goals.

The reason that I wanted to explore failure in what is basically a book about finding success is because each and every individual I spoke with not only failed at many points during their respective lives, but the *most* successful seem to fail on a regular basis. As I culled through memories of conversations, scanned through well over a thousand pages of notes, and listened to hundreds of hours of my recorded interviews, it became clear that how we respond to failure is one of the most important aspects of success—not simply the most interesting from a storytelling standpoint.

Since each individual I interviewed covered many diverse topics,

～～～～ core tenet around each of their stories—

facilitates our ability to achieve success.

〜

IDO LEFFLER OF Yes To, a company I chose to write about in regard to the positive effects of strong corporate culture, even though this story would have been well served within virtually any of these chapters—whether quantifying risk, acting as a disruptive force, or approaching challenges from unique angles—told me about a failure that could have bankrupted the company. When they received their first large order from Walgreens, knowing that Yes To products needed to sell well in Walgreens' stores in order to push the initial trial relationship to a full-fledged partnership, Ido and his team decided to launch a multi-million-dollar print media campaign to help bolster sales, taking out full-page ads in major publications. Despite careful planning, the results were, according to Ido, "disastrous," with the rate of return coming in far below what they had invested in the ad campaign. So far below that it almost derailed the company entirely. "We went into survival mode," Ido told me. "But then, we put *peanuts* into social media and some interesting things began to happen."

And when he said social media, he wasn't just referring to the hot technology of the moment. When hundreds of thousands of people showed up at Woodstock in 1969, it was an event propelled by social media—long before the Internet existed. The Yes To team latched onto a similarly old-fashioned form of marketing by attaching the brand to National Carrot Day, an admittedly obscure holiday that takes place on February third and, spending very little money, organized hundreds of people with "Yes to Carrots" signs to stand outside of NBC's nationally syndicated *Today Show* in fervent support of the company. When it came time for correspondent and weatherman Al Roker to interview a few people in the crowd, which is a staple of the morning program, the only people to choose from were the swarms of self-professed carrot lovers who were sporting both signs and orange clothing in support of the Yes To brand.

This simple concept, a bare-root, homegrown, low-cost media blitz, led to spots on CNN, the *Martha Stewart Show,* the *Today* show, and eventually to features in many of the top magazines and publications in the world. When Yes To launched in Paris, the approach was similar. A massive bus with carrot decor cruised the streets, with free sample bags of products being left on bicycles that were parked all over the city. Rather than giving up or shying away from advertising after spending a substantial amount of capital on a failed print media campaign, Yes To responded with both measured reason and objectivity. Their initial failure propelled them closer to success.

"Anytime I have failed, it can be directly attributable to the failure of *patience,*" Ido told me, emphasizing that response to failure is one of the driving forces in his life—both personally and professionally. By allowing events to transpire in their natural course, Yes To fostered opportunity for growth. Many corporate higher-ups might have internalized a failure of this magnitude and allowed it to function in a destructive manner, either by accepting the defeat as definitive, or by convincing themselves that they simply picked the wrong publications or needed to spend even *more* on the traditional media campaign. Instead, an unemotional response to the poor results of the print media effort led them to a different approach that worked by allowing for the objectivity necessary to take corrective measures. Which is not to say that failing doesn't ever hurt, it's just that successful people learn from it, then quickly move past it.

To illustrate this point even further, Blake Mycoskie, the founder

individual I spoke with, has a unique relationship with failure. He founded a number of other companies before TOMS took off, some of which were successful, and some of which were not. Yet these failures didn't slow him down—they just redirected him.

"After competing on the show *The Amazing Race*, I worked to start a twenty-four/seven all-reality cable TV channel [Reality Central]," Blake told me, "and in a matter of months, I went from being a total nobody in the entertainment industry to doing interviews on CNN and being on the cover of *Variety*. The idea had a really compelling pitch: here I was, a former reality star, starting an all-reality network funded by the winners of big-time reality shows. I was so confident that the idea was going to succeed that I went out and bought a brand-new Porsche—in bright yellow, no less. I felt like I was flying," he confessed.

"And then absolutely everything fell apart. Big personality conflicts started to develop between my partners and me. Team morale began to slip," he said. "And then, in one fatal blow, Rupert Murdoch and FOX announced that they were creating their own reality channel with almost the identical business model as ours.

"The hardest part of this experience was having to call each and every investor and explain to them that their money was gone. What made it even worse is that many of these investors were friends and family members. As an entrepreneur, there is no worse feeling in the world," he shared. Yet Blake rebounded quickly and didn't let this failure keep him down for long.

"One of the best pieces of advice that I've ever gotten is to read the biographies of successful people. As Reality Central was tanking," he told me, "I pored through the biographies of Lincoln, Sam Walton, Richard Branson, Ted Turner, and too many others to count. The common thread among all of these great successes is that every one of them failed—and spectacularly, no less—at some point in their life. As much as it hurt, I realized that failure is an inevitable part of thinking big and going after what you're really passionate about."

Before that, Blake missed winning a million dollars on *The Amazing Race* by less than four minutes—largely because he "refused to stop to ask for directions," as he has joked on several occasions. Prior to that, he had to give up a promising tennis career in college because of a knee problem. It would have been very easy in any of these situations to sit around and feel defeated, to allow failure to become a defining label, but that is not within the actionable set of traits for any successful individual. When Blake's tennis career ended, he started a campus laundry service that ended up becoming a franchise—all because he realized how difficult it was to do laundry while on crutches. The average college student, I suspect, would have responded to an injury or defeat of this nature very differently.

Rafe Furst, the angel investor, business owner, philanthropist, strategic development guru, and world poker champion—who I chose to place in a chapter about modern-day polymaths—*often* invests in companies that end up failing. "Historically throughout the industry, individual angels have averaged five investments per year, and sixty percent of the time they go broke doing so. And yet, angel investing overall has averaged over twenty-five percent annual return, which is better than all other forms of investment over the last twenty years," he wrote to me in an e-mail after our interview. In other words, angel investors *fail* to pick companies that generate positive returns more often than they succeed, but the rate of return cancels out the missteps along the way, and then some.

Extending this line of thinking to poker, the best players in the world regularly lose big pots—it's all part of the game. Sometimes they even will "call" a bet *knowing* that they have likely lost (or failed, as it were), as an intentionally calculated and misleading demonstration of ⌐ ⌐ ⌐ᵣₗₑᵣ ₜₒ maintain a bit of power over a winning opponent

Mike Del Ponte, the theologian turned social entrepreneur, could easily have been written about as someone who operated as a disruptive force or was involved in philanthrocapitalism, asked me—point-blank and very objectively—after making the decision to cease operations at Sparkseed, "What does it mean to go out of business?" I suspect that most people would view this cessation as a failure, but when Mike asked me that question it was clear that *he* didn't perceive it as such. Within weeks, he was sourcing his crowd and moving on to something that is, for him, even more exciting. In this case, as head of marketing for BranchOut, the aforementioned career-based Facebook application that Shawn Fanning invested in and advises. BranchOut launched in July 2010, and during January 2011 it made a staggering leap from 10,000 users to 250,000 users, expanding to Europe in the process.

Here again, because Mike displayed an untraditional response to what most might view as a conventional failure, he was able to use it as a propellant as he rocketed forward toward another success. Interestingly, Mike's perspective on Sparkseed's "failure" played to his advantage. As I was completing this manuscript, Mike called to let me know

86. In fact, some of these failures can manifest as legal issues. At the time of publication, the federal government filed new civil charges against Rafe Furst because of his involvement with Full Tilt Poker, a company not discussed in this book.

that Sparkseed was being acquired and that he would be remaining on its board of directors. "When I announced my decision to shut down," Mike told me, "a number of organizations approached me about acquiring Sparkseed. We selected one that had significant funding and a track record of success in the youth leadership space."

Shawn Fanning's story, although I chose to place it in a chapter about the benefits of being a disruptive force, could easily have fit within the context of the changing face of education (he dropped out of Northeastern), or perhaps used as an example of the value of being a polymath, as his interests and pursuits have spanned across diverse fields and generated millions of dollars for himself in the process. Yet, the truth is, several of Shawn's ventures have "failed." Napster itself could be construed as a failure, as the company encountered many legal disputes over issues of copyright infringement and the free, peer-to-peer version was shut down and declared bankrupt. Yet this "failure" forced the entire music industry to change, launched Shawn's career, and redirected his life—so it simply becomes a question of how we define failure in the first place.

One of my favorite comments regarding failure came from Shawn when we were in his San Francisco loft. When asked about SNOCAP, his follow-up to Napster, a venture that raised millions of dollars and was eventually sold to imeem but was considered to be a failure both in finance and function, he said, "Failure for me was not doing something I was passionate about, and it was in an industry that I didn't know well enough." I was intrigued by how he processed this failure as a learning experience, and by his clear hindsight. "SNOCAP started for the wrong reason. I didn't believe entirely in the approach," he confessed, "but I didn't have the foundation or background to disagree with these people who had experience. I sort of became a mascot. It was really stupid of me to jump into something right away. I learned so much from that. I did everything right with Napster when I was building it, and then I did everything wrong with the next one. But I worked with great people. That's the one thing," he told me. Shawn's perspective pertaining to failure is perfectly in tune with nearly everyone I spoke with in the sense that he recognizes failure as a key to learning and growing, both personally and professionally, and the fact that we need to separate single instances of failure from our measurement of self-

A YEAR SPENT interviewing people and writing about success was culminating rather ironically, as I spent the final weeks of this process homing in on the concept of failure. The entire journey, exploring and mapping a route to success, was about to conclude with one final interview that would focus on defeat. Extending this irony even further was the fact that I wanted my key interview for this chapter to be with a person so big and so successful that calling on such a person to discuss failure might have seemed, at least on paper, to be absurd. Making this task even more challenging was the fact that, as previously mentioned, I wanted this individual's story to serve as a drop test not simply for how we process failure, but for all of the tenets previously outlined as well. But it was only after I had selected who I thought would be the perfect candidate, meticulously prepared material, and then conducted the interview that I realized just how protracted the irony of my choice really was. Even though it was unplanned and completely coincidental, I was not only closing a book about success with a chapter about failure but I had opened with a chapter about a company that makes shoes, and the final interview turned out to be about shoes as well. Yet despite this unintended structural fluke, it became clear that the real irony lies in the fact that neither company really has much to do with shoes at all.

〜

SELLING SHOES ONLINE does not, at the onset, sound like a brilliant, billion-dollar idea. In fact, to be honest, it sort of sounds like a relatively bad idea. How do you sell something like shoes, which are difficult to size and fit at your local mall, let alone over the Internet, and turn it into a global phenomenon—especially if you are selling brand names that are available elsewhere? So, I figured if someone could reach the top rung of success with a "bad" idea, there was no better company to use as a drop test for these success tenets than Zappos.

Tony Hsieh (pronounced *Shay*), the now legendary CEO of Zappos, sold his first company, LinkExchange, to Microsoft for $265 million at age twenty-four. Zappos itself was recently acquired by Amazon for $1.2 billion, and Tony wrote a number one *New York Times* best-selling book called *Delivering Happiness* that details not only the rise of Zappos, but his life philosophy as well. I asked Tony, who is widely regarded as one of the greatest business leaders of this generation, to talk to me about failure. And he agreed.

Since much of the Zappos story is well chronicled in his book, as I prepared to interview him I wanted to ensure that we covered the topic of failure in a way that he hadn't already written about—at least not in depth. But before delving into what Tony Hsieh had to say about failure, I first wanted to backtest all of the success tenets outlined on these pages by projecting them through the lens of both his personal story and the story of Zappos.

On the education front, Hsieh, while he attended Harvard, barely went to class. Bored, and consumed with entrepreneurial endeavors and projects of personal interest, he found ways to get decent grades without having to actually show up. In fact, Hsieh has gone on to openly challenge people to take the money they might spend attending college and use it to start one company each year for four years instead, suggesting that such an approach might provide a better education and result in more opportunities for the same investment as a bachelor's degree.

In terms of taking on and quantifying risk, Hsieh quit his first job out ~~~~~~~~~~~~ during the dot-com boom, a job

They declined ~

passed. Most would say that turning down $1 million for a company that had been in existence for four months is a risky move, but turning down $20 million? Finally, two years later, Tony and his partner sold LinkExchange to Microsoft for $265 million. He was twenty-four years old and had proven himself not only as a successful entrepreneur but also as an expert in valuation, dogged perseverance, and at quantifying risk as well. As chronicled in his book, Tony also assumed massive risk by continuing to support a bootstrapped Zappos with his own money. Based on the current valuation of Zappos, it is clear that he was once again correct in his risk assessment.

With regard to company culture, Zappos is well known for being one of the best companies to work for in the world. As a single example of how different this culture really is, when new team members complete their training, during which they are paid, they are then offered two thousand dollars to quit—just in case they are not completely committed to the company or the position isn't the right fit. The Zappos team members are treated like members of a large family rather than as mere employees. Tony has built a company culture at Zappos that revolves completely around "happiness," as the title of his book suggests—his happiness, customer happiness, and employee happiness.

While it has been established that the nuance of corporate culture is often difficult to capture without actually experiencing it, Zappos employees wear what they want to work, spend significant time together outside of the office, and when the company was acquired by Amazon for $1.2 billion in late 2009, all Zappos employees got a free Kindle and a 40 percent bonus on top of their annual salaries. Tony and his team built a management and leadership program based on proven psychological research—employees are happier if they have friends at work; receive small, frequent promotions; and feel like they are part of something bigger instead of simply a cog in the machine. And he built the company this way not just because he knows that happy employees are more productive. This, for him, is not simply a corporate policy—it's a life philosophy. Justifiably, in 2011 *Fortune* magazine ranked Zappos at No. 6 on their annual Best Companies to Work For list.

Tony and his team approached every aspect of the business from unique, often counterintuitive angles, choosing to divert the majority of the resources that a corporation like Zappos would typically spend on advertising into facilitating a world-class customer-service experience instead. Stellar customer service would generate word of mouth, they reasoned, thereby creating a loyal customer base and building sales while outperforming and outshining any brand development that might result from advertising dollars. And they were right, as proven by the fact that in less than a decade Zappos is now generating over one billion dollars in annual revenue. The employees in their call center don't read from scripts, and Zappos imparts no time limit on phone calls to the center from their customers (while I was writing this, unfathomable as it may seem, an internal company record was set with one customer-service call lasting over seven hours). Zappos allows customers up to a year to decide if they want to keep or return each pair of shoes, and if after 364 days it is determined that the shoes aren't quite right, as long as they are in new condition, the customers are granted a full refund—with free shipping in both directions, of course.

Zappos is built on a business model defined by networking. The leader-
~~~~~ ~nd their now massive customer

~~~~~~~~~

team. By facilitating a world-class, "no-rule" customer-service exper-
ence, they are able to build relationships and trust with the people who
matter most: their customers. In essence, Zappos has replicated the
small town, neighborhood shopping experience and customer-
shopkeeper relationship online.

Continuing this litmus test, Tony and the Zappos team unquestionably
acted as a disruptive force, not only within the niche shoe industry, but
in the retail space as a whole. So much so that consumers have changed
their buying practices, are increasingly taking their dollars online
instead of to the local store or mall, and have changed the expectations
they have for other retailers they purchase from as well. Zappos was
such a disruptive force within the online shopping realm, in fact, that
the retail giant Amazon, in an effort to keep them from becoming an
even a larger competitor, forged an alliance with Zappos by buying the
company.

Tony embraced the approach of a polymath, translating the technology
skills and dot-com mind-set he developed during the late nineties while
building LinkExchange and then applying these same skills, with
unparalleled success, to the seemingly polar opposite world of online

retail merchandising—refining his life and corporate philosophy of "Delivering Happiness" along the way. Taking the energy-driven, almost feverish pace of high-tech companies and applying it to the traditionally slower-paced, staid environment of shoe sales in a counterintuitive manner allowed for the explosive growth of Zappos. Further, by applying his personal values and documented psychological research pertaining to happiness and blending it with corporate ethos, Tony and the Zappos leadership team were able to create their own formula for success.

Tony and the Zappos team act with passion on a daily basis, and have done so from day one. In fact, it is their passion that jettisoned them to the position they are in today. They became so passionate about Zappos, the customer-service experience, the building of a self-contained company that followed its own rules, and the formation of a like-minded family of individuals that the company succeeded seemingly against all odds. For Tony and his partners, Zappos was never simply about shoes. It was *about* passion and happiness. Not just for them, but for everyone who came into contact with the company.

Which brings us to failure.

⌐

WHEN I CALLED on Tony Hsieh to discuss failure, I was quick to explain that it wasn't because I thought that anyone could somehow possibly construe that *he* was a failure. But rather, since failure is such a close cousin to success, I suggested that nobody would be more intimate with it than someone who had achieved as much as he has.

In his book and in interviews, Tony has openly discussed the fact that after he took over as CEO of Zappos—a company he had initially invested in and then stepped in to run—they were going through growing pains. After exhausting all other options, being turned down for venture capital and lines of credit, he had to liquidate many of his own assets in order to keep the company going, or else let it go under. Years into it, in a final move to keep Zappos afloat for an additional six months, Tony sold a large loft affectionately known as "Club Bio" for 40

... ... for—despite family, friends, and

considered ...

"I think a lot of people can view failure as a negative and label themselves as such," he tells me. "People with an entrepreneurial spirit view failure as part of a process—not a permanent label. Don't view failure as a character flaw," he advises, which is how many of us internalize failure. "If you get a cold, for example, you don't view yourself as being permanently sick. It's something you have to get through, then move on. I view failure in the same way."

Capturing this sentiment in an even more focused manner, I referenced a line from Tony's book that I found to be quite compelling. "Even if Zappos failed," he wrote, "we would have known that we had done everything we could to chase a dream we believed in." So, I asked him, what would he have done next? Was there a plan in place? I was attempting to identify a post-failure thought process. How do successful people anticipate failure and plan ahead?

"I would have just moved on to the next idea or opportunity," Tony says. "I didn't know what that would be at the time, of course, but something else would have presented itself or I would have thought of something. That's part of the Silicon Valley culture," he tells me matter-of-factly. And it makes complete sense within the mind-set of successful people. If he had already had an exit strategy, it would mean that he was entertaining the *possibility* of defeat. An orientation that, in and of itself, would have made failure more likely. The odd, yet perfect, combination of psychological underpinnings that support success includes the belief that failure is so normal that it is neither feared nor anticipated. Then, when and if it does occur, it is sourced for value and simply stripped of all power by being dismissed. "Failure is not a badge of shame, it's a rite of passage," he tells me casually, and I proceed to write it down three times.

Failure is not a badge of shame. It's a rite of passage.

As far as specific, individual failures at Zappos, the learning process continued with each failure. I ask Tony about one of their early partnerships with a shipping company called eLogistics, which went horribly wrong rather quickly and involved a truck turnover on the side of the highway with 20 percent of Zappos merchandise being lost in the process. I am curious as to whether this was perceived to be a failure, a positive learning experience, or both.

"ELogistics was a subsidiary of UPS, so we didn't research as many companies as we probably should have," Tony tells me. "So in that sense you could say we failed. We had no warehouse experience, so we didn't know what to look for. We assumed that they would be good and provide a better experience for our customers—so our intention was in the right place. Partnering with eLogistics is a failure that stands out. We should have done more research." But Tony's mind works in an analytical and unemotional way that allowed him and the Zappos team to rebound from the truck spill and the merchandise loss, demonstrating how the lessons learned more than made up for the temporary defeat.

"If we hadn't gone with them first, we wouldn't have known that Kentucky was the right location for our shipping and warehouse. We were in San Francisco at the time, and we might have chosen a lesser-quality or less-efficient local warehouse. So even though the eLogistics decision was a failure, it led to a great success because we learned from it," he continues. "Were it not for that mistake, we never would have developed the efficient warehouse system that we have now. It exposed us to the right location in order to provide the best service to our customers." Kentucky's central location, and the fact that the Zappos warehouse is a mere fifteen minutes from the UPS main shipping hub, is part of what enables Zappos to fluidly execute their world-class cus-

order something from Zappos

reflective of a

business and working toward the greater good of the company.

"It was a failure in the sense that we should have been managing toward proper head-count numbers all along, instead of being backed into a corner," Tony tells me. "Each department manager went through their team and analyzed who and what we needed to keep and what was holding things back. Eight percent was just a random number—we didn't set out to lay off eight percent specifically—that's just what the number came out to. The failure there was that if people fell into the 'unnecessary' category, we should have noticed it and identified it beforehand," he acknowledges.

Recognizing that most people, especially young people who are navigating the career marketplace, are more likely to join the conventional workforce than start their own company, I ask Tony for his advice to young people looking for jobs during periods of high unemployment and the concept of finding what we are "meant to do," so to speak. "Reconsider what your options actually are," he emphasizes. "Twenty to thirty years ago, the only option was to get a job. Now, with the Internet, there are so many options. Find your passion and pursue it. That doesn't necessarily have to mean starting a company at all," he is quick to point out. "Know what you want and what you're good at— you will find a way to make it work and succeed."

And what about those who *do* want to assume some risk and pursue a passion or perhaps start a business of their own? "If you want to do something a bit more difficult, like become an artist let's say, Seth Godin,[87] for example, makes the point that all you need is one thousand 'fans' who would be willing to spend a hundred dollars a year with you. That's a hundred thousand dollars and is more than a comfortable living. Then just add one fan a day. If your passion is underwater basket weaving, and you're great at it, you will find an audience and a way to make a living and be happy," Tony tells me. Even within spaces where failure is exponentially more likely because of the very nature of the endeavor, Tony has a practical and pragmatic viewpoint. He is so comfortable with failure that his ability to emotionally desensitize and objectify it makes seemingly impossible tasks appear not only possible in the theoretical sense, but actionable and viable as well.

On a lighter note, referencing a story touched upon briefly in his book, Tony tells me about a learning experience he had when he was in college. "I had been skiing since second grade. In downhill skiing, you turn the skis abruptly at ninety degrees to stop. This, however, is not a good idea when it comes to ice skating for the first time. I went ice-skating when I was in college and made the mistake of thinking that because I was good at something that was similar (skiing), that I would be good at that too. I wound up getting stitches," he says, laughing in retrospect. The takeaway, however, is notable on a broader scale. "Just because we are good at one thing does not mean that we are going to be good at something that seems to have commonalities," he tells me.

Early in our conversation, before we even got into a discussion about failure, I asked Tony about his definition of success. I wanted to understand how someone with the business acumen of Tony Hsieh defines

---

87. Seth Godin is a celebrated entrepreneur, business leader, and the author of *Purple Cow* and *The Dip*, among others.

the term, so I could better frame his perception of failure. "My parents, for example," he says, "like a lot of Asian parents and families, define success as status—having money is better than not having money, having an advanced degree is better than not having one, and so on. My

[text obscured] to lose everything tomorrow, would

[text obscured]

found. His definition of success, in this example, is simply [text obscured]. For him, success is not starving or being eaten by a saber-toothed tiger. Extrapolating from this perspective, we almost *can't* fail unless we are no longer breathing. If our definition of success is this minimal, logic could lead us to believe that we might never reach a level of success that someone like Tony Hsieh or any of the other people in this book have. But the opposite is true.

> *This minimal expectation removes all barriers*
> *that might impede the ability to achieve on the*
> *highest level, not the motivation to do so.*

↜

SO WHAT DO the successes, failures, and unique journeys of these individuals, companies, and organizations have to do with us?

Absolutely everything.

After nearly a year of observing, spending time with, and learning from these highly successful individuals and their collective initiatives, it became clear that there is a set of skills, a mind-set, and a behavior pattern that comes naturally to some and that others can readily learn to model. In capturing the cumulative wisdom of the leaders profiled on the pages of this book, it is my hope that many of us can use this information as an accelerant for change in our own lives. If what we want isn't being offered to us, we should go out and create it for ourselves.

When we don't think of "what we do" as a job, we are freed up to find "who we are." We can kindle the most dramatic change—change that will enable us to define and achieve success on our own terms—if, rather than looking for a conventional job, career, or lifestyle constrained by traditional norms and expectations, we harness the opportunities afforded to us as a result of a drastically altered global landscape and a shift in generational expectations as we set out with an objective that is altogether different.

Creating a life.

OPENED THIS BOOK by stating that we have landed in a new place. I pointed to the seismic technological advances that have altered who has access to the information and knowledge that was once held under lock and key and disseminated almost exclusively by academic institutions and the corporate elite. The almost unlimited access we now have to self-education has drastically facilitated our ability to explore new areas of interest, to find our dream jobs, to start new businesses, and to facilitate global change without relying on what were once the traditional paths to do so, and has, in many instances, reduced the underlying costs and accelerated the speed with which an idea can be vetted or a new venture can be launched. I further argued that these technological advances have collided with a shift in generational expectations and cultural values that have collectively resulted in substantial change within the career marketplace. I opened this book by stating that as a result of these changes, even though we might not realize it, we are a generation holding an unprecedented amount of power.

Yet despite these massive changes, for young people, most advice about finding a job or building a career revolves around the technical details of writing a résumé, the imperative of the right font, or the critical importance of résumé length. And as we fret over whether a résumé should be confined to one page or spill over onto a second, whether or not to include that we were a lifeguard or worked in retail one summer, as we debate over what to wear to an interview and worry about the right haircut or whether or not jewelry is appropriate, we are missing a chance to focus on what really matters. Even though we face tremendous pressure over what college we attend, what courses we take, our grade point average, or what to major in, when we stumble out of school and look for a job, we sometimes forget to make sure that we try to get the *right* job in the *right* field and at the *right* company. As we seek the affirmation of landing *any* job and long to bask in the honor bestowed upon the newly employed, it is easy to forget in all the stress of the job hunt to get the *right* job— especially in times of high unemployment. We don't understand how much power we have to completely change the trajectory of our lives.

The reason that career-seeking advice and job seekers' attention often revolves around trivial details is simple. These are the actionable and tangible things that are easy to grab hold of, so we assign them inordinate value. Often, if we don't get a job we applied for, we look at our résumé, reconsider the font, and question its page length. We blame the blue shirt we wore to the interview, decide that we should have chosen a different tie or that some jewelry would have been better than no jewelry. And these details do matter, of course, to a degree. Pajama pants, a Mohawk, and facial piercings are clearly not the best choice for a job interview in finance. But I think most of us already know this. We all know that within the parameters of acceptability the length and the font of a résumé, the lifeguarding, the blue shirt, the job in retail, and the brown tie are all fine. But since we don't know what else to do, and feel a lack of control, we assign great importance to the wrong things.

The reason that this happens defies logic. We spend years preparing for college, tens or even hundreds of thousands of dollars attending school, and then we often send out résumés and apply for jobs that we hardly understand at companies we know little about, and take the first position offered. We don't craft a life, but rather we take what we can get and then settle in and try to make it work. We often race to employ-

... ...ting there quickly is more impor-

aren't easy to ...

find a job we love in a career that matters. What this book is designed to do is just that: help each of us focus on the broadly applicable, hard-to-hold-on-to constructs that can truly effect change in our lives, so that we can effectively and efficiently build a personally crafted life and find *that* job and *that* career—the one so well suited for us that we almost didn't dare dream about it.

If we apply the lessons culled from the stories in this book to our own lives in a stripped-down, uniquely personalized manner, we can achieve the goals we didn't dare dream about and reach these destinations faster and with more efficiency, as we simultaneously build lives we can actually get excited about. To accomplish this, we need to respond to ordinary events in extraordinary ways, listen to our gut, accurately assess and then appropriately assume risk, follow our passions, and allow those passions to direct, kindle, and fuel our success. As a means to create opportunities for ourselves and to unearth creative solutions to existing problems we also need to be willing to self-educate, release ourselves from the restrictions of conventional thought, challenge established paradigms and institutionalized norms, approach problems

88. In 2010 the Conference Board reported record low job satisfaction. Only 45 percent of Americans were satisfied with their jobs, and the younger the worker, the lower the reported job satisfaction.

and opportunities from unique angles, and act as disrupters in order to bring our own set of experiences and knowledge base to divergent fields. If we recognize the long-term value of the right job, at the right company, by calculating the exponential personal and career growth that avails itself to us when we work with like-minded individuals in an affable environment, and then set out to build and source powerful networks by recognizing the facilitators around us, we can connect with the right people and forge mutually beneficial relationships of value, altering, in a substantive way, the trajectory of our lives. If we embrace capitalism not as a textbook economic theory but as a tangible, accessible, leverageable, and powerful tool available to everyone and anyone interested in starting a business to create sustainable and palpable change, we can become part of a movement that is branding social entrepreneurship and profit with purpose as the trademark of our generation. In so doing, we can both satiate our inherent altruistic tendencies and fill the coffers of need as philanthrocapitalism becomes the face not only of a generation, but also of sustainable change. And perhaps most important, if we put ourselves out there and dare to fail, we can ultimately find a level of success and self-satisfaction on a scale that might have previously seemed impossibly grandiose.

If we think about the success tenets offered here as practical, functional tools—if we think of them as simple intellectual machines, just like a wheel and axle, a lever or a wedge—they can facilitate success as they offer us mechanical advantage, as they make the work of finding and building a life and career easier by altering the magnitude and the direction of the force we exert. Armed with these few simple career-building tools, we are given the ability to accomplish a disproportionate amount of work—to lift unimaginable weight. We need to think about these tenets as the simple machines of life and career planning, and recognize that each of us will use them uniquely, in different combinations, with a different focus, in different venues, with different end goals.

If we look around and see how often, and how differently, a wheel and axle are used, alone or in combination with a lever or a wedge, we can look around and see the varied applications of social networking and risk too. If we think of failure as a lever, self-education as equivalent to a job-search pulley, building a powerful network as the functional wheel and ⸺⸺⸺ ⸺⸺ as a disrupter or following the

become the com⸺

generate more, and to facilitate work-life flow—just like a wheel and ⸺ facilitate movement. Armed with a few career-based simple machines extracted from the toolboxes of highly successful individuals, we can literally change the trajectory of our lives.

In closing, I offer you one final success story. One final run-through of the success tenets presented on these pages. This time not backtested by the experiences of a CEO of a billion-dollar company. This time simply filtered through the ordinary story of a recent college graduate on a job search. Someone who wasn't attempting to start a company or solve a global humanitarian issue; just someone looking for an entry-level position right out of college. Someone perhaps just like you. Someone who is at the forefront, the very beginning, of immeasurable success.

〜

SHE WENT AGAINST the grain in college. She didn't pick a traditional major, like economics, education, or premed. Instead, she wandered a bit. Seemingly lacking career direction, she sampled courses from every academic department—took some art classes, poetry, African dance, a bit of math and statistics, Arabic I and II, Chem 101. She got a broad liberal arts education that was about as unfocused from a career stand-point as it could be. It might have seemed to an outsider that she was intentionally selecting courses that would make her, in the conventional marketplace, virtually unemployable. When finally forced to declare a major during the first semester of her junior year, she looked at the classes she had taken to date, and the only viable major that would allow her to graduate on time was International Studies. So she checked it off, signed up with an adviser, and learned that her school mandated that since the major required proficiency in a second language and she had studied French, her only option was to declare her focus in African Studies. Not exactly what she had expected when she enrolled in college, but she embraced it. She spent a semester abroad in Paris, where she didn't particularly like the electives offered, so she petitioned the admin-istration for permission to create an independent study of her own—she chose, of all the unlikely things, to study perfume.

She wandered a bit more. She took courses in wine appreciation and exotic fare as she continued to read esoteric articles on olfaction. A col-legiate polymath wandering the academic woods, she was pursuing everything that she loved—but worried late at night that her job pros-pects upon graduation were not likely to be very promising. She went to Italy for a summer session and studied the Italian language, Roman architecture, oenology, medieval history, and the culinary arts. She fin-ished the semester by writing a paper on the importance of Moroccan saffron to the spice routes. She became obsessed with ethnic cultures as they related to fragrance and olfactive traditions. She wrote her senior thesis on something even more obscure, titling it, *Osmology and Spiri-tuality of Scent in Disparate African Tribes*.

She didn't make her way over to career services her senior year, and she didn't write a résumé. In fact, she had no idea what she wanted to do, so she avoided the "job topic" altogether. She had no clue how to put her educational background and varied interests into play. The prospect of finding a job, let alone a life, loomed as entirely overwhelming. She was great at math, but found finance boring. She loved chemistry, but in the laboratory and classroom she found it to be a bit dry. She loved modern art, jazz piano, slam poetry, food and wine—and felt that if she couldn't be creative she would shrivel up and die. Her biggest fear at ~~. . . . .~~ ~~. . . ld and up~~ living a real-life version of the

copyedited and proofed, she still had no clue where ~~to send it~~. ~~. . . . .~~ took a bit of a risk, "sat at the wrong table," so to speak, and joined a professional organization in the fragrance industry that she happened to stumble upon while searching for jobs. At first she was a little reticent because of her age, but she gathered her courage and attended perfume-sniffing events for industry professionals in New York City and stepped into a multi-billion-dollar international industry full of people with interests just like her own. While attending these events, she introduced herself to as many people as she could, told them about her passions and varied interests, built a network, made connections with key members of the industry, engaged them with interesting scientific and cultural olfactive factoids whenever she could, and followed up with e-mails. Eventually she was offered a one-day-a-week internship at a small fragrance distributor, where she wrote product copy, translated documents from French to English, and learned a lot about fragrance marketing—and herself.

Over the next few months, through her newly minted connections, she was called in for interview after interview for sales and marketing positions at various fragrance companies—but she didn't get a single offer. They loved her passion and self-education, but there was always someone a bit more qualified, someone with a few years of experience in sales or marketing or a degree in statistics or chemistry. Inwardly, she was secretly relieved. Some of these positions looked a bit dry. Too much spreadsheet, too little sensory exploration. Too much like *The Office* and those dreaded paper sales—at least for her.

Desperate to move out of her parents' house and to move on with her adult life, she took *any* job—a job about as wrong for her as you could imagine—at a company with bad culture in a field she didn't care about. And at that moment she hated her life. But this failure redirected her. It reinforced her passion and reminded her how important it was that she find the right position at the right company. She refused to let this setback settle in or to let it define her. She left that position, but followed the wrong job with the wrong internship, where she worked for minimum wage and suffered maximum boredom. She had an impressive job title, but in reality she was expendable—just another overqualified intern earning and learning nothing as she gift-wrapped books and tweeted about macaroons. All the while, she continued to send out résumés targeting both large fragrance houses and niche boutique companies all over New York, as she read everything she could find related to the science and culture of scent. Then, after almost a year of job searching, she walked into an interview at the creative fragrance design center of one of those multinational fragrance houses, sat down with the head of fragrance development, and unexpectedly had an interview conducted almost entirely in French. She was prepared. She was asked to sniff perfume samples, to identify and describe the fragrance notes. They discussed viniculture and botany, perfumers and artists—from Jacques Guerlain to François Coty and Olivia Giacobetti, from Coco Chanel to Jean-Michel Basquiat and Christopher Brosius. She landed the job of her dreams.

She now wakes up every day and *runs* to work. Her boss recently asked her to present her esoteric thesis on olfactive practices in disparate regions of the world. Seasoned employees took notes when she spoke; they stayed afterward to learn more about the tribal olfactory typologies of the Serer-Ndut from Senegal, the Dassanetch of Ethiopia, and the Dogon from Mali. Legends in the industry have taken her under their wings. She works with some of the most famous perfumers in the world, sniffing and writing about fragrance and art and food, working in creative development, surrounded by orchids, oakmoss, labdanum, and sandalwood. She speaks their

artists, African tribes, oenology, and gustation. Everything together for her, as it did for the others in this book, and she excels at her job.

She hasn't sold a company for fifty million dollars, but she has found a career and a life she loves. She is twenty-three years old and has never been happier. She is living her waking dream, which for her is infused with the scent of tonka beans and immersed in sensory-rich creativity. She looks down into her bag, next to the fragrance bottles and the passport, the shea butter and the saffron, next to the wrong major, the insecurity, the esoteric reading material, and her renaissance walk through the academic woods, and what she sees is her dogged perseverance. Her personal risk, disruption, and passion. Her immeasurably self-directed *self*-education that afforded her an entrée to the perfect career. She can see these tools sitting there as clearly as if they were a wheel or pulley, a lever or a wedge. She was fueled and directed by passion, propelled by her willingness to take risks, to follow her gut, to educate herself, to approach a field from an unusual angle, to sit at the wrong table, to build a network and embrace a multidisciplinary approach, to find the right job at the right company, and to accept nothing short of extraordinary for herself.

It makes no sense on paper. She seemingly did everything wrong, and yet she found herself standing in the foothills of extraordinary success. Just like many of the other individuals profiled on these pages.

Change the details, and any one of the
stories in this book could be yours.

We have landed in a new place.

Shake the world.

I WOULD LIKE TO express my deepest love and appreciation to my family—Mom, Dad, Kate, Mackenzie, and Daisy. Thank you for your unconditional love and encouragement. I consider myself to be the luckiest son and brother in the world. To Tom, Sarah, Chris, Doc, Nancy, Heather, and the rest of my extended family, I could not ask for a better, funnier, or smarter support system.

To my agent, Andrea Somberg at the Harvey Klinger Agency, thank you for your guidance and insight, and most of all for believing in this project from day one. To Adrian Zackheim and David Moldawer at Portfolio/Penguin, thank you for supporting this sketch of an idea from the get-go. Jillian Gray, thank you for your unrelenting confidence and input as we completed this process. To Will Weisser, Allison McLean, Jackie Burke, and the rest of the Penguin team, you have been nothing but insightful, supportive, and patient. I thank all of you deeply.

I would like to express a special thank-you and my greatest respect to all of the amazing individuals who took time out of their incredibly busp schedules to meet with me. You invited me into your offices, your homes, and your lives. I appreciate your candor, honesty, and commitment to the greater good. I learned more in the last year than I ever could have imagined, and there were many times during this process when I had to pinch myself just to ensure that I wasn't dreaming. I am genuinely humbled by the work that you do.

To Jared Shahid, Will Read, Matt Twichell, and Rachel Margolin, you help me keep things in their proper perspective on a daily basis and I am incredibly lucky to call you my friends. I aspire to be more like each of you. To Anthony David Adams, I am grateful every day for your visionary thinking, your inspired work, and, most importantly, for our friendship.

A special thank-you to Elliot Bisnow and the Summit Series team—being around you inspires me to be my best when I wake up each morning, which is the greatest gift anyone could ever ask for. To the brilliant folks at Effigy Farms, much of this would not have been possible without you—my deepest gratitude for all of your generosity and wisdom. Josh Zabar, you are a true samurai. Thank you for everything, especially the eggs.

To anyone whose story did not make the final edit, I apologize and can assure you it was only an issue of space and editing. I easily could have written five books with the material and content you so graciously provided. I am proud to call many of you my friends, and this book would not have been possible without each one of you and the world-changing work you are doing. You are all making the planet a better place.

This has been a life-altering year for me. I abandoned my corporate shackles and met with hundreds of people from all walks of life. Each of you has contributed to my constantly evolving worldview, and I will be forever in your debt. Finally, to anyone and everyone I am leaving out—you know who you are—my sincere thanks.

Your student,
James